THE
VALIANT
NELLIE
McCLUNG

THE VALIANT

NELLIE McCLUNG

SELECTED WRITINGS
BY CANADA'S
MOST FAMOUS SUFFRAGIST

Barbara Smith *and* Nellie McClung
foreword by Dave Obee

VICTORIA | VANCOUVER | CALGARY

Heritage House Publishing Company Ltd.
heritagehouse.ca

CATALOGUING INFORMATION AVAILABLE FROM LIBRARY AND ARCHIVES CANADA

978-1-77203-146-1 (pbk)
978-1-77203-147-8 (epub)
978-1-77203-148-5 (epdf)

Edited by Lara Kordic
Proofread by Merrie-Ellen Wilcox
Cover and interior book design by Jacqui Thomas
Cover photos: portrait of Nellie McClung, appearing in *Farm and Ranch Review*, January 2, 1930
Frontispiece and chapter opener photo: Nellie McClung, circa 1905–1922, by Cyril Jessop,
Cyril Jessop / Library and Archives Canada / PA-030212

The interior of this book was produced on 100% post-consumer recycled paper, processed chlorine free and printed with vegetable-based inks.

We acknowledge the financial support of the Government of Canada through the Canada Book Fund (CBF) and the Canada Council for the Arts, and the Province of British Columbia through the British Columbia Arts Council and the Book Publishing Tax Credit.

20 19 18 17 16   1 2 3 4 5

Printed in Canada

For my great-granddaughter, Isabella Lilly

CONTENTS

W hy, after so many years, do the words of Nellie McClung continue to resonate with Canadians? Why do her opinions still matter so much? Why does the mention of her name still inspire us?

Perhaps it's because she helped make Canada a better place. Perhaps it's because Canadians are living better lives today because of her work, and without even knowing about the debt they owe to Nellie McClung.

The raw genealogical data shows that McClung was born in Chatsworth, Ontario, in 1873, and died in Saanich, British Columbia, in 1951. But really, that data does not mean much; it does not provide a sense of her determination and her dedication, and her commitment to achieve results despite overwhelming odds.

That women have the right to vote, as an example, is a given these days. More than a century ago, before men had granted that right, McClung and the other women's suffragists faced an enormous struggle. It would have been easier to give up, and to find a cause that would seem more attainable.

Our Nellie did not give up. And later, when she joined with four other Albertans in the fight to have women recognized as persons under the law, she did not give up. McClung felt her cause was just, and she stayed with it, despite the odds.

Nellie McClung was a suffragist and a strong believer in the temperance movement. She was a politician and a reformer. She was an engaging orator and a prolific writer, with several books, magazine articles, and newspaper columns to her credit. She had a keen wit, which she used to great advantage when pushing for social change.

McClung was highly regarded in her lifetime, but her work has had much more recognition in the years since her death. She was featured on a Canadian postage stamp in 1973. A park in Edmonton bears her name, as do schools in Alberta, Manitoba, and Ontario, as well as a library branch in Saanich. She is remembered in the Famous Five monuments in Calgary and Ottawa, which in turn were featured on a fifty-dollar bill.

In 1954, the federal government declared that McClung was a person of national historic interest. In 2009, all members of the Famous Five were declared to be honorary senators—the first people to be so designated. Three of her former houses are heritage sites, and two more have been preserved at a museum in Manitoba.

While her books, such as *Sowing Seeds in Danny* and *In Times Like These*, have remained in the public eye, many of McClung's newspaper columns have been all but forgotten. Her early ones were collected in two *Leaves from Lantern Lane* volumes, but her later columns were neglected until the Victoria *Times Colonist* began reprinting them in 2014.

This book makes the columns accessible to a wide audience again, and will ensure that McClung's later work will be enjoyed for many years to come.

These columns included here were written at a remarkable time in history. The world was in turmoil, with events in Europe demanding attention around the globe. Her calm, rational point of view was what Canadians needed at the time.

Many of McClung's words seem as relevant now as when she wrote them, which indicates that a logical approach based on respect for human rights is timeless. In a few cases, her writing and her ideas seem dated, but that should not come as a surprise, given the passage of time.

It should also be no surprise that the work of Nellie McClung continues to inspire our nation, as it has for more than a century. She was one of the most influential Canadians of the first half of the twentieth century, and her work helped shape the Canada of today.

The Valiant Nellie McClung brings some of her most significant writing into the public eye once again. It's about time.

—Dave Obee, Editor-in-Chief, *Times Colonist*

PROLOGUE

January 28, 1914. *The weak winter sun set early in Winnipeg, Manitoba, but the palatial Walker Theatre was alight with activity. A din of expectant chatter rippled through the sold-out audience. Onstage behind the curtain, people and props were shuffled into place. The house lights dimmed, the crowd settled, and the performers drew in their collective breaths. A moment later the curtain rose on a presentation destined to change the course of Canadian history.*

Nellie McClung sat at centre stage in the role of Sir Rodmond Roblin, the Conservative premier of Manitoba. She was a natural for the part, a clever mimic with an innate sense of dramatic timing. And she loved the limelight. Nellie's friends and colleagues from the Canadian Women's Press Club and the Political Equality League were also seated on the stage, posing as members of parliament.

No detail had been overlooked. All the women wore black choir robes over their evening gowns. Two girls, one of them Nellie's fifteen-year-old daughter, Florence, were dressed as parliamentary pages. The girls waited quietly in the wings until their services—delivering messages between the members or bringing them glasses of water—were required. Other women played the roles of men presenting creative proposals to the "premier."

Ripples of laughter greeted Nellie's responses to various propositions set before her. The declaration that men should always be clad modestly in public, for instance, delighted the crowd.

Then, when a petition was presented requesting that men be granted the right to vote, Nellie blustered in a perfect imitation of Premier Roblin's distinctive speaking style: "I believe a man is made for something higher and better than voting. Men are made to support families. Politics unsettles men and unsettled men means unsettled bills, broken furniture, and broken vows, and divorce!"

Nellie let the absurdity of her statement register with the audience before continuing, still mimicking Roblin's style: "When you ask for the vote for men, you are asking me to break up peaceful, happy homes, to wreck innocent lives, and this is something I will not do."

Gales of laughter and thunderous applause echoed through the theatre. Nellie McClung had used her signature wit and sense of humour to make her point. She received a bouquet of roses from the Manitoba Liberal Party, the government's official Opposition. Her life in provincial politics was set in motion.

The next day, newspapers ran long articles under bold headlines describing the women's performance at the Walker Theatre. The Winnipeg Telegram called the evening "highly enjoyable," and added, "The cause of women may not be so hopeless after all and the vote may not be so far away as one might be inclined to fear." The Winnipeg Free Press wrote, "A sold-out house at the Walker Theatre last night testified to the keen interest taken in the activities of the Political Equality League."

After the roaring success of that evening, the women gave the performance once more in Winnipeg and again in Brandon. They played to sold-out audiences each time and, more important, they had made their point: denying women the vote on the basis of unfounded claims that suffrage would lead to the destruction of the family and unravel the moral fabric of society was as absurd as denying men the vote for those same reasons.

Clearly, the message struck a chord with the public and the political powers that be. Two years later, in 1916, Manitoba became the first Canadian province to grant women the vote. This was the first significant step in the long process of granting voting equality to all women, and all Canadians—a process that would take several decades to come to full fruition.

Today, Nellie McClung is remembered as a leader in Canada's suffrage movement, a political pioneer, and a member of the esteemed Famous Five who took on the British Privy Council in 1929 to have women declared legal persons under the law. Yet Nellie was more than her activism, and more than her charismatic public persona. She was a remarkably down-to-earth person who came from humble beginnings and stayed true to her beliefs all of her life.

Letitia Ellen Mooney *came into the world on October 20, 1873, on a hardscrabble farm near Owen Sound, Ontario. She was the youngest child of John Mooney and Letitia McCurdy, immigrants from Ireland and Scotland, respectively.*

From the time she was able to speak, Nellie had a great deal to say for herself. This delighted her father, with whom she shared a stronger bond than she did with her mother. John Mooney particularly enjoyed his daughter's ability to mimic people—especially her mother's prim and proper sisters.

When Nellie was seven, the family moved to a homestead near Wawanesa, Manitoba. The prairie was now hers to explore. Over the next few years, the family farm prospered, as did those of their neighbours, and the community banded together to build a school. Ten-year-old Nellie began school in a red and grey homespun dress that caused her great embarrassment, but her life was opened up forever when her teacher, Frank Schultz, taught the inquisitive girl how to read and write.

Mrs. Mooney worried about her youngest child's impetuousness. The girl not only read voraciously, but even worse, she loved to entertain people. At one point she shocked her mother by declaring that she intended to become an author and never marry. Later, encouraged by the much-admired Mr. Schultz, Nellie softened her stand only enough to include becoming a teacher so that she'd have a regular income while she wrote part-time.

To that end, in 1889, at the age of sixteen, Nellie applied to attend normal school (teachers' college) in Winnipeg, following in the footsteps of her older sister Hannah. Like Hannah, Nellie was a dedicated student and excelled in her classes. In January 1890, Nellie returned home with a teaching certificate and accepted a position at Hazel School, a one-room schoolhouse near Manitou, Manitoba.

Nellie enjoyed the children she taught and encouraged them in every way she could. In addition to their regular lessons, she introduced them to outdoor sports and planned pageants for them to present to the community. But there was a dark side to this small town that Nellie was not sure how to deal with. At first, she noticed that some of her students weren't thriving academically or socially like the others. After making inquiries, she realized that the common factor in their homes was alcohol abuse. Nellie shared her concerns about the children growing up in such an unstable environment with a woman she greatly admired: Annie McClung.

Annie was a Sunday school teacher and the wife of the new Methodist minister in Manitou. She was also a member of the Women's Christian Temperance Union (WCTU), an international organization founded in Ohio in 1873, which opposed the manufacture and sale of alcohol. Annie was vivacious and outspoken, and she soon became something of a mentor to young Nellie, who prophetically declared her to be "the only woman I would want as a mother-in-law."

Nellie agreed with the WCTU's conviction that alcohol abuse devastated families. She also strongly supported the organization's initiative aimed at granting women the right to vote. She and Annie began speaking out publicly against distillers. This was Nellie's first exposure to the heady world of activism, and her experience entertaining her father with imitations of her aunts and producing school pageants served her well, for Nellie had become a gifted, eager, and effective public speaker who fully understood the power of humour, even in a serious address. She would occasionally remind her audiences that, despite what some husbands might think, the initials WCTU did not stand for "Women Constantly Tormenting Us."

Nellie moved to Manitou and boarded with Annie McClung, her husband, and their two younger children. Wes, the McClung's oldest child, *was away at university but came home occasionally for holidays. He was an athletic, intelligent, and sensitive man who had been raised by a forward-thinking mother. As she describes in her autobiography* Clearing in the West, *Nellie in her typically forthright fashion "went to the store where Wes was employed and purchased a fountain pen with [her] last three dollars. He had no chance of escape after that."*

After Nellie's beloved father died in January 1893, Nellie realized that life was short and should be lived to the fullest. She upgraded her teaching certification and began teaching at the school in Treherne, Manitoba. The McClungs had also relocated there, and Nellie continued to board with them.

Wes returned home after completing his studies, and he and Nellie courted for four years, during which Wes operated two pharmacies and Nellie continued to teach and speak out in favour of temperance and women's rights. When Wes proposed, he assured Nellie that marriage wouldn't mean that she would have to give up her dreams for the future. She accepted his proposal, and the two were wed on August 25, 1896. They moved into a four-room flat above one of the drugstores Wes owned in Manitou. A couple of years later, they moved into their own house, where Nellie began to write the story that would eventually become her first (and internationally bestselling) novel, Sowing Seeds in Danny.

In 1897, Wes and Nellie's first child, John Wesley (called Jack), arrived. Two years later their only daughter, Florence, was born, followed by Paul in 1902, and Horace in 1906. Nellie thrived on the busyness. Sowing Seeds in Danny *was published in 1908, followed by* The Second Chance *in 1910. Nellie was also active in the WCTU, where she was in great demand for her skills as a persuasive public speaker. With every speech she promoted temperance and social equality.*

By the time Mark, the McClungs' last child, was born, in 1911, Nellie had made a name for herself as both an author and an activist. Wes, however, was feeling stressed by the responsibilities of the pharmacy business. He took a job in Winnipeg as a salesman for Manufacturers Life Insurance. Nellie dreaded leaving the life she'd created in Manitou, but by August of that year the family was happily living in Winnipeg.

Nellie wasted no time in making a new home in the city for herself and the family. She helped form the Political Equality League and joined the Canadian Women's Press Club. It was through the latter organization that she met a visiting Emmeline Pankhurst, the leader of the British suffragette movement, who strongly influenced Nellie and broadened the scope of her activism.

At the time, immigrant women made up a large portion of sweatshop labour in Winnipeg, toiling in inhumane conditions for hours on end. Determined to bring this to the attention of Premier Roblin, Nellie and Edna Mary Nash paid a call to the premier's office and insisted that he accompany them to one of the factories where women worked in noisy, dark, filthy rooms. Roblin went along with the two women, but apparently he could not tolerate the environment for more than a few minutes before he fled from the building. Nellie and Mrs. Nash had succeeded in making the most politically powerful person in Manitoba aware of the severity of the workers' plight and the immediate need for improved legislation.

Emboldened by this apparent success, Nellie and her fellow activists approached the premier's office and officially requested that women be granted the right to vote in provincial elections. Roblin turned them down. Not to be deterred, Nellie and her colleagues hatched their plan of performing a mock parliament—which culminated in Nellie's historic impersonation of Premier Roblin at the Walker Theatre on January 28, 1914. The energetic young woman was in her element.

Meanwhile, Nellie's books were selling well, and she travelled to many provinces to give readings. She always used these opportunities to campaign for social justice and gender equality, and she was a hit wherever she went. Of course it didn't hurt that she was entertaining, personable, intelligent, and always beautifully turned out. Audiences—primarily made up of middle-class, middle-aged married women with children—couldn't get enough of her. She spoke eloquently about the appalling working conditions in factories and stressed the importance of temperance in society, stating that one in five boys would grow up to become an alcoholic. "Do you have a boy to spare?" she would ask her audience.

In the midst of Nellie's literary success and growing popularity, the world was going to war and her family was uprooted again. In 1915, Jack McClung, just eighteen years of age, joined the fight overseas. Nellie and Wes were heartbroken; they knew he was too young and too sensitive to survive the war unscathed, but the young man was determined. Within weeks of Jack's departure, the family suffered another upheaval when Wes's employer transferred him to Edmonton. Nellie worried that she hadn't been able to do all she could for the province of Manitoba, but she found Edmonton to be a vibrant city, full of hope for the future, and soon felt completely at home. She established herself there by joining the Edmonton Equal Franchise League and the local chapter of the Canadian Women's Press Club. She also became friends with Alice Jamieson and Emily Murphy, the only women magistrates in the Dominion.

Nellie continued to speak to groups across Canada about prohibition and social equality with the aim of protecting the lives of women and children. Her energy created enough momentum that Nellie and her peers forced a plebiscite in Alberta. If the majority of voters agreed with the stand against the sale of alcohol, Conservative premier Arthur Lewis Sifton would have to enact that legislation. Nellie pulled out all the stops. She organized a march in downtown Edmonton.

On a hot July day in 1915, Alice Jamieson, Emily Murphy, Nellie McClung, and twelve hundred supporters assembled at the agreed-upon meeting place. But rather than marching, most of the women huddled in small groups along the sidewalks, too timid to step out onto the roadway. As determined as always, Nellie approached a woman in the crowd who was leaning on a crutch. Together the two strode out to the middle of Jasper Avenue, Edmonton's main downtown street. Their example was enough to encourage the others to follow. The following year Alberta became a legally dry province.

With Nellie's help, in January 1916, the pro-suffrage Liberals were elected in Manitoba, which became the first Canadian province to *grant women the vote. Saskatchewan followed in March and Alberta in April. Nellie, Emily Murphy, and Alice Jamieson celebrated by buying new hats and having their photo taken together.*

The political tide had turned, and Nellie McClung's industry and ingenuity deserved much of the credit, but any joy she might have felt at the victory was blunted by her constant concern for Jack's well-being overseas and the knowledge that she still had obligations to fulfill. Even so, Nellie had become more than just an author and an activist; her intelligence, wit, and charisma had propelled her to celebrity status. Her personality drew people to her so powerfully that she became fondly known as "Our Nell."

In 1916 and 1917, Nellie toured the United States speaking on behalf of the National American Association of Women's Suffrage. She took her teenaged daughter, Florence, as her travelling companion. The two made an appealing combination and were enthusiastically received wherever they went. People flocked to Nellie's presentations, and the local press was always full of adulation. She covered an incredible forty cities in roughly six weeks, at each stop delivering passionate variations of one or other of the speeches promoting gender equality that were her stock-in-trade. Also in 1917, women in British Columbia and Ontario won the right to vote.

In 1918, Prime Minister Robert Borden invited Nellie along with her friend and fellow Edmonton activist Emily Murphy to represent Alberta at the Women's War Conference in Ottawa. This was the same year women's suffrage was enacted federally. The two travelled east to speak out about equal pay for the women who had stepped in to fill men's jobs while they were fighting overseas. They also pushed to introduce access to technical training for women who wished to join the workforce but weren't qualified.

When the Great War ended later that year, women left the jobs they'd held while the men were away. Many of those men returned injured both physically and mentally, and one of those men was twenty-two-year-old Jack McClung. Nellie noted that her son was a "changed man," and the McClung family dynamic shifted awkwardly to accommodate this new, more sombre Jack, who was most likely suffering from post-traumatic stress disorder.

In 1919, Nellie was heartened when William Lyon Mackenzie King became leader of the Liberal Party. To her mind, the controversial leader was the man Canada needed in order to move ahead after the havoc that the war had wreaked on the world. She admired him so greatly that when she decided to run for a seat in Alberta's provincial legislature in 1921, she ran as Liberal candidate despite the fact that her beliefs were more closely aligned with United Farmers of Alberta (UFA). The UFA won the election that year, but Nellie made history by winning in her riding just five years after she'd won the right to vote. True to her form she supported legislation that made sense to her, even when it meant voting against the Liberals. Her close friend Irene Parlby was a UFA cabinet minister, and the two women worked together effectively to promote their causes.

As important as these milestones were, it is necessary to mention that the right to vote was not extended to everyone. Canadians of Asian descent (men and women) were excluded from the vote to some degree until 1948. Inuit people got the vote in 1951, while First Nations women and men were not granted full voting rights until 1960. There is no doubt that Nellie was an enlightened and progressive thinker, but, like all of us, she was a product of her time—a time when Christian women of British descent were far more privileged than many others in Canada. Nellie and her fellow activists were not immune to the racist attitudes of the early twentieth century. Their fight for women's rights was driven by a vision of Canada that was predominantly white and Christian, and although Nellie was greatly concerned with the plight of immigrant workers and later supported the acceptance of refugees from Europe, the specific interests of women of colour were largely ignored by the early suffrage movement.

In 1921, Nellie was the only female delegate from Canada to attend the Ecumenical Methodist Conference in London, England. She was unimpressed by more than a week of meetings, later declaring that the highlight of one particular evening was the jewellery worn by the speaker's wife and that the speaker himself knew "some cracking big words." Although the conference was disappointing, London was not. Nellie stayed on for an extra month, thoroughly enjoying being a tourist. Before boarding the ship back to Canada, she visited France, where she paid her respects at battle sites from the Great War.

During Nellie's four years as an elected politician, there were changes in the McClung household. Manufacturers Life Insurance transferred Wes to their Calgary office. While he and the rest of the family made the move, Nellie stayed behind in Edmonton to fulfill her political obligations. She commuted back and forth when she could, but the situation was stressful. In 1923, Wes became suddenly and critically ill, and Nellie took a leave of absence from her political post to stay with the family in Calgary while Wes recovered at a medical facility in Banff. That same year, prohibition was repealed in Alberta. Nellie took the reversal with resignation and determination to push on.

During the 1926 provincial election campaign, Nellie ran as a Liberal candidate again, this time in Calgary. She was narrowly defeated and took the loss in stride, maintaining that having fewer political responsibilities would allow her to spend more time writing.

And write she did. In the next five years she wrote five books, all with themes of women's rights or temperance or both. At the same time, she was active in every women's organization in Alberta. Although she was now in her early fifties and had arthritis and a heart condition, Nellie was nowhere near ready to slow down. In fact, she was about to face another enormous political battle.

Lawyer Eardley Jackson, *the man who initiated this next important change, had absolutely no wish to further the cause of women's rights. His goal was to discredit Magistrate Emily Murphy because, on July 1, 1916, she had ruled against his client. Jackson refused to accept her ruling, claiming that she could not legally hold the position of judge, because under the wording of the British North America Act (BNA Act) she was not a "person."*

The man's utterance shocked Emily Murphy, but when she researched his pronouncement she found he was correct. The BNA Act read: "Women are persons in matters of pains and penalties, but are not persons in matters of rights and privileges."

Murphy then investigated further and discovered a clause in the BNA Act that allowed any five British subjects to approach Parliament and ask for clarification of any portion of it.

On a late summer day in August 1927, Magistrate Murphy invited four women to a meeting at her home near the University of Alberta: Henrietta Muir Edwards, author of the book Legal Status of Canadian Women; *Irene Parlby, an Alberta cabinet minister; Louise McKinney, a former member of Alberta's Legislative Assembly; and "Our Nell."*

Magistrate Murphy presented them with a letter she had written to the federal government asking for an interpretation of the offending clause in the BNA Act. All five women signed the letter and sent it to Prime Minister Mackenzie King. Years later, Nellie said she wished she had kept a copy of that letter because "Mrs. Murphy was a master craftsman in the handling of a pen. She had no difficulty in finding the apt word."

Despite the letter's clarity, or perhaps because of it, no one in Ottawa was anxious to be its recipient. The prime minister referred the missive to the minister of justice, who in turn sent it to the Supreme Court of Canada. Late in April 1928, the five signatories, and the rest of the country, knew the decision. Astonishingly, women were not, in the legal sense, persons.

25

In a stellar example of circuitous logic, Chief Justice Francis Alexander Anglin explained that the BNA Act was enacted in 1867, when there were no women serving as elected officials, and therefore the Act excluded women in its definition of persons. This meant that women could not be appointed to posts such as magistrate, or to the Senate.

The five activists, on behalf of women across the country, approached the next court of appeal, Britain's Privy Council. Finally, on October 18, 1929, the Privy Council announced that women were indeed persons under the law.

Although Emily Murphy had been the driving force behind this important change, she received very little credit for her efforts during her lifetime. By the time the petition had reached the Privy Council, the five women's names had been alphabetized and so the document was recorded as "Edwards versus Canada."

None of the Famous Five—as the women came to be known—was ever appointed to the Senate (although all five of them were appointed posthumously as honorary members in 2009). They did receive some accolades, though. On June 11, 1938, the Association of Business and Professional Women of Canada presented a plaque honouring them that was to be placed in the Senate foyer. Only Nellie attended the unveiling. Emily Murphy, Henrietta Muir Edwards, and Louise McKinney had already died. Irene Parlby chose not to leave her rural Alberta home for the occasion.

At the presentation, Nellie looked resplendent in an evening gown and new shoes that she later admitted pinched her feet. William Lyon Mackenzie King admired Nellie greatly, as she admired him, and he spoke briefly in his blustery style honouring the Famous Five. Nellie responded with her usual warmth, wit, and humour. The transcript of her response follows:

Madam president, Mr. Prime Minister, fellow Canadians, I desire to thank the Prime Minister and the president [of the Association of Business and Professional Women of Canada] too, and I thank the Prime Minister still more for the kindness he showed to our little petition when it was just little scrap of paper going around and not very welcome any place. I also wish to thank Newton Wesley Rowell for his kindness in taking our petition to the Privy Council and I also wish to thank Lord Sankey for his glorious decision, so clear cut and unmistakable and unanswerable. [*laughter from the audience*]

I would like very much tonight, dear friends, if I could express the . . . minds not only of the five us but of all people who have advanced the cause of women by means seen and unseen. The great unnumbered and unremembered and unknown people who have done so much for us, the people whose names will never appear in the paper, the people whose names we'll never know, because it has been a long task, it has been an epic story, this rise of women. They had to begin from so far down. Women had first to convince the world that they had souls and then that they had minds and then it came along to this political entity. [*more laughter*] And the end is not yet. We feel that there are still people who would sign the minority report. Now I do wish to pay my tribute of love and admiration to the other four women whose friendship I enjoyed and treasured, for their loyalty and for their love and for their steadfastness, for their wonderful companionship. Mrs. McKinney, Mrs. Muir Edwards, and Mrs. Parlby . . . and particularly I wish to give my tribute of praise to our undaunted and indomitable and incomparable leader, Emily F. Murphy. She didn't care who got the honour. She was never one to care who got the vote of thanks. She would joyfully pin a medal anytime on somebody else, and you know dear friends, I can't help but saying now that we're all here together that we would all be able to accomplish a great deal more if none of us cared who got the credit, and tonight if she is listening from some other [of] the islands of the bliss, I'm sure that there is no person who will hear the words of this ceremony with a lighter and a merrier heart.

Seventy years after the personhood decision, on October 18, 1999, a larger-than-life bronze statue of the Famous Five was unveiled on Parliament Hill in Ottawa. The installation captures the women celebrating their victory. Sculpted by Barbara Paterson, it stands near the statues of Queen Victoria and Queen Elizabeth II and is one of the most visited sites on the Hill. Nellie is shown holding up the newspaper with headlines proclaiming that women are, after all, persons. Irene Parlby is beside her, while Henrietta Edwards raises a teacup to toast their success and Louise McKinney clasps her hands together in glee. Emily Murphy, who initiated the entire movement, stands beside an empty chair, gesturing for the visitor to sit and join them. Many people accept Magistrate Murphy's invitation and have their picture taken with the esteemed group. There is an identical statue by Paterson in downtown Calgary that was unveiled by then–Governor General Adrienne Clarkson in October 1999, and an equally impressive statue in Winnipeg, sculpted by Helen Granger, was unveiled on June 18, 2010.

By the early 1930s, Wes's retirement was drawing near, and the McClungs decided to make a move—this time away from their beloved Prairies to the mild climate and picturesque charm of Victoria, BC. For the first few years they rented accommodation, but once Wes retired they began to look for a permanent home. In 1935, they found and bought a property they called Lantern Lane. This would be their dream home for the remainder of their lives. It was from this home, surrounded by her lovingly tended garden, that Nellie spent five years writing a nationally syndicated newspaper column.

Nellie's loyal readers, many of whom had followed her career since the early days of her activism, now looked forward to reading this remarkable woman's thoughts on everything from interior decorating and gardening to women's rights and the looming spectre of war. The following pages offer just a taste of Nellie's prolific writing during this last phase of her incredibly varied career. The majority of the columns included in this volume have been republished in recent years by the Victoria Times Colonist newspaper, whose predecessor, the Daily Times, originally brought Nellie to Vancouver Island readers between 1936 and 1942. Other columns included here were found in Leaves from Lantern Lane (1936) and More Leaves from Lantern Lane (1937). For the most part, the columns appear exactly as they were originally published, with only occasional minor edits made for the sake of clarity or brevity. Nellie's voice has been splendidly preserved. It is worth noting, however, that some of the opinions and turns of phrase in Nellie's writing reflect the time in which she was living, as well as her position of relative privilege. Although we are living in very different times, Nellie's determination and lifelong commitment to promoting fairness and equality are remarkable, and we are all living in a more just society because of her efforts.

29

< Barbara Paterson's Famous Five sculpture in Calgary. D & J TRUMBLEY

i. Life at Lantern Lane

The McClungs moved to Vancouver Island in the early 1930s, but it took a few years for the transplanted Prairie couple to find a permanent home and put down roots. The house hunt was discouraging until one dull, dreary day in January 1935, when they took a drive north of Victoria to the rural area of Gordon Head and found an abandoned 1.5-storey house on several acres of land overlooking the ocean. They called the house Lantern Lane. The property became their dream home, the place where Wes spent his retirement, where Nellie began the last phase of her career, and where the couple celebrated their fiftieth wedding anniversary. Lantern Lane— the house and its garden, as well as the surrounding neighbourhood —was always the backdrop (if not the subject) of Nellie's newspaper columns, which she began writing in 1936. The place seemed to ground her and give her inspiration, whether she was writing about topics close to home or global in scope.

Part of life at Lantern Lane was its surrounding community, and at the centre of that community was the local church, St Aidan's. Nellie was a devout Christian—as is evident in many of her columns— but other factors tied her to the church. She staunchly believed in the power of groups of people banded together for a common purpose, and the church was another organization with the potential to get things done.

> Lantern Lane, undated but from Nellie's time. SAANICH ARCHIVES, #1981-023-004B

Nellie became a church elder at St. Aidan's, the first woman in Canada to hold such a post. She had no desire to become a preacher herself (though her columns sometimes read like sermons, and her son Mark once commented that she would have made an excellent minister), but she campaigned passionately for women to be ordained and accepted as spiritual leaders. For Nellie, religion and women's rights went hand in hand, which is evident from the beginning of her participation in the temperance movement. Her involvement with St. Aidan's only strengthened her faith, and gave her the sense of community that had perhaps been lacking since she and Wes relocated from the Prairies.

The following columns all have a strong sense of place—specifically, Lantern Lane and its surrounding neighbourhood, but also Vancouver Island and the West Coast as a whole. Nellie's adopted home is a source of delight, introspection, and the bonds of community.

"EVEN IN THE COBWEBBY LIGHT, IT HAD A CERTAIN BEAUTY."

January 19, 1935, was a perfect day to look at a house with the intention of buying. None of your beguiling, sunshiny, wheedling days that lowers one's sales resistance and makes almost any place in the country appear inviting. No, it was a rough, grey day, with razor blades in the wind and white caps on the sea. Not only that, but in spite of the cold, there had been downpours of rain from the iron-grey clouds that had obscured the sun for weeks. Indeed I had a sinking feeling sometimes that the sun might never shine again. There was a finality about it all, a thick, settled, stubborn greyness.

We were not enthusiastic when we heard of another country place. No one could be enthusiastic about anything. The whole country, east and west, was in the grip of the worst winter since '79; but we had come to Vancouver Island to buy and we drove out the six miles to see the place. Nobody spoke. It was better to do anything than sit in the lounge of the hotel and look out at the slanting rain between us and Elbethel Chapel, or watch the motionless old ladies in their purple and grey nightingales, just sitting watching the fire, with no sound in the room but the ticking of a clock on the mantle. The hotel advertising mentioned that it was "a quiet place," and we found it had not exaggerated.

We drove out the six miles to Ferndale Road and saw the house standing well back from the gate, "For Sale" signs leaned against the fence. We turned off the road and drove between two rows of cherry trees up the lane. The land sloped to the east and south, and even in the cobwebby light, it had a certain beauty. The house, a dark green, shingled semi-bungalow, looked old and comfortless but any empty house on a dull day of drizzling rain looks like a woman who has just washed her hair.

We got out of the car and went to the front of the house and up the steps to the veranda and then something happened which seemed like fate.

The sun came out! A sudden, unexpected flood of light ran over the fields and down to the sea. It lingered on the bright red roof of a white house on the right, almost hidden in the trees; it caught the wings of a wind-mill on a water tower below us; it lighted up the wall of evergreens across Ferndale Road to the north; it glittered on a white sail out on the sea. And then it was gone and the woolly greyness rolled back. But we had seen the beauty of Gordon Head in that one bright, revealing flash.

The house had been empty for several months. Rain had filled the chimney and soaked through the plaster, pools of water stood on the floors and the smell of wet lime added a touch of desolation. But we could see that the floors were straight, the windows opened easily on pulleys, and there were plenty of them, there were three fireplaces, and upstairs off one of the bedrooms was a sunporch, looking out to sea. Its windows were broken—old torn blinds hung crookedly, water stood on the floor, but none of these things mattered. The little place had the right feel. It was friendly and welcomed me in. Windows can be made whole, old blinds can be changed to new ones. I knew I would have bright draw curtains on the windows and the ceiling would be painted white, and I would put a light on the south wall, and my desk and filing cabinets would fit in, and I'd have a long hanging shelf for a few books above my desk—and when I looked up from my work I would see the sea! I would look out on a world of great waters!

Downstairs in the den there was a cobblestone fireplace and on the mantle I found a name, "John Fullerton," and then I was sure this was the house for me, for was not my grandmother one of the Fullerton girls away back in Dundee?

And now we have been here a year and the little sunporch is mine. I have the draw curtains and the light over my desk. Above the garage door we have a ship's lantern, which throws a welcoming beam of light on a dark night, down the lane between the cherry trees and gave us the name "Lantern Lane." There are no street lights out this far, of course, but no one minds that. When we visit the neighbours in the evening we carry a homemade light made by sticking a candle in the curving side of a jam-tin and carry it by a wire handle fastened to the two sides, which lets the light stream out in a circle on the road ahead of us. At first we used a flash-light, but it was a feckless thing that went out one real dark night when we were out and left us to come home by the Braille method. But there was something pleasant in that, too, for it made us think of the times we found our way home over Manitoba trails on moonless nights, with the wolves howling.

Across Ferndale Road there is a woody path called "Banshee Lane" which leads to the sea, and when I first turned in at this dark green archway and walked on its carpet of leaves below the trees, breathing the clean earthy odours of moss and fallen trees, and saw the path ahead of me stippled with sunshine and heard the myriad sounds of the little wild creatures and knew this bit of wild wood was mine by right of an ancient inheritance, I had all the exaltation of one who has come into a fortune. "Banshee Lane" is a public path, by the generosity of one of the old inhabitants, and it can never be widened into a motor road. Great arbutus trees with their smooth red boles that make one want to stroke them, symmetrical maples and evergreens so high that looking at them becomes a good exercise for neck, the kind that must be taken carefully, make up the woods, with hard old yews, descended probably from the trees from which Robin Hood and his men made their bows. The shiny-leafed Oregon grape carpets the ground and in their season, white and pink mayflowers abound with the glorious crimson of the flowering currant. There are flat logs to sit on beside the path and open grassy places, whose brightness smites the eye after the dim greenness of the thick woods.

The welcoming feel of the house on Lantern Lane has been sustained and confirmed by the whole neighbourhood. Not once have we rued the haste with which we bought it. Our neighbour to the east, whose wind-mill caught the rays of that first flash of sunshine, is a bulb-grower from the Sicily islands, who came here twenty-five years ago, with a wagon-box full of bulbs. Now his fields of daffodils and tulips often appear in pictures and the blooms go far and wide. But the commercial side of it fails to interest him. He is a grower and a lover of flowers for their own sakes and is not disposed to bargain as to their disposal. When a new neighbour comes in, he is ever ready to give assistance and practical help. When he says he'll send you over a few bulbs—you may get five thousand. The men and women in this neighbourhood who spent their youth here owe him a debt, for he made it his business to see that they all learned to swim and they will tell you now how Mr. Edwards would leave his team standing at the head-land at any hour of the day, to go down to the sea and give a lesson to anyone who came. His "Sea Cadets" are men and women now and they are imparting the love of the sea, learned from him, to their own children. So his good deeds go on, an unfading entry on the right side of life's ledger.

Then we have for our neighbours, on the other side, two retired Hudson's Bay people who spent many years in the North and from them we hear fascinating tales of Indians and missionaries; of the uncanny intelligence of the wild things; and of how the beaver families separate at the end of the first year, by some inexorable eugenic law, all the males going upstream and the females downstream.

There are three Irish sisters, belonging to an old and aristocratic family in the County Dublin, who live in a house hidden in trees but who would no more think of cutting one down than of bobbing their hair. From them I get Irish newspapers and we talk of Don Byrnne and the horse races at Curragh.

There is another neighbour who makes it her care to see that the sick are visited and the needy clothed. She has a quilt in the frames perpetually (not the same quilt) for some poor family. She is the Good Angel of Gordon Head, whose "light goeth not out at night."

The house, whose red roof, almost hidden in trees, gleamed its welcome that first day, belongs to a Winnipeg friend, whose fine old back cat, "Major," ended his glorious career just before we came. "Major" was raffled at a Red Cross meeting in Paris, as soon as his eyes were opened, in the first days of the war and was won by a Canadian war-bride who lived in hotels and who carried him past hotel clerks in her muff. "Major" came to Victoria when the war ended; when his people moved back to England he was brought to the red-roofed house in Gordon Head and lived the life of a country gentleman, and died full of years and honours.

At the corner of Tyndall Avenue and Ferndale Road there is a lovely garden whose beautifully wrought iron gates are always open and over its green lawns we are all welcome to wander, by the generosity of the owners, who are also prairie people. In the spring there are flowerbeds of red tulips, shaped like baskets, and little crocuses in yellow, white and purple star the grass. Over the low stone wall runs a lacy green creeper that changes to pink and red as the season advances. And near the house are stately maples and cypress, and among them are deodar (which to me existed only in Kipling stories), the deodar with its spreading lower branches resting on the ground and quite at home in Canadian soil.

There are two men in our neighbourhood who came in to Vancouver on the first transcontinental train fifty years ago, and from them we hear stories of the romance of railway building and of the rugged men who planned the conquest of the mountains. There

is a pianist from one of the prairie cities, who plays for us every Friday night in the winter, Chopin and Mendelssohn and Bach, in her huge living room. The log fire burns down into coals, then into embers, and the last bus changes gears on the hill and we know very well that it is twenty minutes to twelve, but, under the magic of her fingers, all sense of time has gone.

We see on fine days, to the south, the snow-capped Olympics over in Washington. The snowy top of Mount Baker looks down on us, over the shoulder of San Juan Island across the Strait of Haro, and the lights of the city six miles away form a pale illumination on the southern sky.

Surely, I said to myself, here is a place to dig in and be at peace, where no harsh sounds break into one's reverie. The day breaks gently over the sea; the dogs bark softly, or not at all. Life comes on like distant organ music. Vancouver Island takes you as you are, without comment, because it knows what you are does not really matter. So you can go ahead and say what you like. Write to the papers if you wish. No one will be disturbed or bothered, for the real business of life will go on anyway. The salmon will run and spawn and die; the purple and white and yellow aubretia will cover the rocks; the broom will pour of its gold in May; and the Olympics across the straits will glow at sunset with cool radiant fire.

It was my intention to write a continuation of *Clearing in the West* as soon as we were settled here. I had seen the beginning of so many things: women's struggle for political equality, the rise of women's clubs, the heroic struggle to eliminate the liquor traffic and its disastrous sequel. I had been at so many "first" meetings, and had known the women who had shaped opinion in Canada, many of them gone now, too soon. I wanted to put into words what I knew of these women who had been too busy making history to write it.

But I couldn't write it. I was too comfortable. I had not grown accustomed to a spring that comes in February, with snowdrops and violets and wallflowers. The anaesthesia of beauty had me in its clutches.

I had laughed at the story of the two rival editors from the prairie, who had come to this Island and had happened to settle quite near to each other. In the little town in which they had lived in Manitoba, they had fought each other in the gallant red-blooded way that belongs to that exhilarating climate. They had never missed a chance of reviling each other and they did it with a tartness of invective that delighted their readers. Now, they live side by side, amicably sharing a party line telephone. They talk across the fence about tent caterpillars and sprays and fertilizers, and exchange confidences on how their arteries are hardening. They send each other gifts of roses and violets wet with dew, new potatoes and Swiss chard. When I heard about the Swiss chard I could have wept, remembering what bonnie fighters they once were. If any gift from the vegetable kingdom had passed between them then, it would have been a sheaf of poison ivy, tied with barbed wire.

Now something like this has come over me and I want to talk about the lavender bed from which I cut the old stalks to make way for the new ones; or the wallflowers that are making a golden brown glow against the new stucco on the house; and the daphne, with its faintly fragrant berries; and the laburnum tree at the gate that will soon swing its golden lanterns in the wind.

"THEY HAVE SOMETHING IN THIS LITTLE CHURCH WHICH CAUSES THEM TO WALK IN THE LIGHT."

> 1936

Three miles from Lantern Lane and under the shadow of Mount Tolmie, stands the little country church to which we belong—a little white church with a wrought iron lamp above its door, on which appears the word "St. Aidan's." I was curious about the name and was glad to get a clipping from one of the members in which the story was told of the young missionary who had gone out from the monastery of Iona in the seventh century. It seems that the word in Northumbria had been slipping for some time and the last two incumbents had come back to the home base, discouraged and dismayed, reporting that the Northumbrians were a wild lot, as fierce as their own wild beasts, and nothing could be done for them. Then Aidan volunteered for service and went out alone.

One day he returned in triumph to his Alma Mater, reporting that the Northumbrians were not as black as they had been painted, for the "cause" was flourishing in many places; and from the efforts of this young man, who laboured with the Northumbrians all his life, the banners of the Cross were firmly planted in that wide region which comprised all the territory from the Humber to the Forth. He died on the thirty-first day of August, 651.

"St. Aidan's" has an ecclesiastical taste on the tongue and makes a more dignified name for a church than "First" or "Central" or "Sixth Avenue."

Lately we have had an uncommon sight on a Sunday morning to see confetti on the steps and a great arch of flowers in front of the altar. The explanation given by the caretaker of "folks from town, who phoned out for flowers and came out in three cars, just because they like our little church, being as it reminds them of the church they attended back in Ontario," is easily understood, for we felt the charm of St. Aidan's, too, the first time we entered it. It has an atmosphere of peace and beauty and remoteness from this troublesome world. St. Aidan himself would be pleased with it, especially since we got our windows.

The windows came from England many years ago, for the home of one of our Premiers [Sir Richard McBride]. Three years ago, the minister of St. Aidan's was a caller at this lovely home and admired the windows. The mistress of the house said she cared but little for them, they were too formal and old-fashioned for a home and really should be in some church. Plain glass, she said, would suit her better. Whereupon the minister, with a sudden wild plan forming in his mind, said he would take her at her word and give her plain glass for the stained glass.

St. Aidan's Board of Managers confirmed the bargain and there began at once a season of activity. The Ladies' Aid went into action on all fronts. Teas, bazaars, rummage sales, home-cooking sales, autographed quilts. It was not merely the exchange of windows, the whole church had to be gone over, massaged and manicured. It had to have its floors scraped, its roof painted, a new system of lighting; the beautiful windows had to have the proper setting. One of the members, a builder, spent his evenings carving an oak pulpit and communion table.

One bright sunshiny day, all was ready and the new St. Aidan's was opened and re-consecrated to the "service of God an community." The windows, one in the north over the front door, have a design of autumn leaves, flowers and birds in subdued colours that glow and

42

gleam in the filtered light. So exquisite is the workmanship that if you look closely you will see a spider spinning his web.

The minister, whose quick thinking started the crusade for a more beautiful St. Aidan's, left a year ago for a larger church in a neighbouring city and another came to us. Again the beneficent spirit of St. Aidan's brooded over the little church under the hill, for our new man, in addition to his many gifts, is a gardener of ability and imagination and quite early in his ministry he called out the troops to make the outside of St. Aidan's as beautiful as the inside.

He set the men digging and rolling and planting and now St. Aidan's sits up proudly on a terraced lawn and rejoices in hedges and rock plants and borders of annuals; while behind the church in the grounds of the manse are fruit trees and a lily-pond, with ferns and gold fish. Two golden holly trees flank the new cement walk and now the autumn flowers in blues, yellows and golden brown hold back the gloom of the rainy season.

Naturally, we are all proud of our lovely little church, though proud is not exactly the right word. Our people come to church gladly and they come long distances, many of them. Market gardeners, dairy farmers, chicken farmers naturally work long hours but they manage to go to church, and to accommodate the whole family and some of the neighbours they drive their trucks. No one drives away with empty seats in his car and a car is not considered full if the doors will close.

The neighbour whom I called the "Good Angel of Gordon Head," and who knows everyone in the church, is the unofficial traffic manager. When the service is over, she will tell you whom you are to take home. She can flash one glance over the congregation and compute the motor needs as quickly as that. If the morning is rainy, some cars may have to make two trips, but no one minds that. We like to stay awhile and talk anyway.

St. Aidan's finances in a simple way. The Elders and the Board of Managers meet once a month and everyone comes, for we have a good time. There are no threatening letters from banks or finance companies. The financial secretary's report is a model of simplicity.

The envelopes and loose collections bring in enough to pay the minister and caretaker and they are paid weekly. We may have six dollars on hand to start the new months or we may have only three. One month we had ten dollars left over and we gave a bonus to the caretaker, for he had done extra work around the garden. That left us with five dollars, which was plenty. We are not hoarders.

We are very proud of our choir but we are not narrow or mean, for when singing visitors come to our neighbourhood, we invite them to sing for us. Our choir leader is a Yorkshire man and he loves the swelling melodies of the old hymns and leads us through "Belmont" and "St. Agnes," "Wiltshire" and "Olivet." We are glad to hear again the rolling cadences of "There is a land of pure delight, where saints immortal reign," sung to the old tune of "Lyngham," which brings us back in memory to the joy of our first love.

Our Sunday school meets before the morning service, in a new part of the church, built at the time of the Window Upheaval and called The Assembly Hall. It's a snug little place with an open fireplace, which has a welcome feel now that the colder weather is here. The superintendent is a young man (whom the children call by his first name) who has the gift of talking seriously to children and yet gripping their attention.

I often look at this room full of children, well-brushed and comfortably dressed, and think with admiration of the tired women who get up early on Sunday morning to get their families into this state of soap-and-water righteousness. There is one family that lives two miles or more from the church, whose members come in at intervals. The mother evidently releases each child as soon as he is ready (she probably tried the plan of putting the clean ones on chairs to wait but found it did not work). So they arrive one-at-a-time, shiny-faced, punctuating the opening exercises ...

I met the mother at our annual picnic and was surprised to see how young and light-hearted she is. She won all the women's races. I asked her how it happened that she was such a good runner. Had she chased jack-rabbits in her childhood? She said she had always been a good runner and added, "You have to be with eight children to chase after!"

The attendance of babies at our Sunday school has been large this year. Little girls who have young sisters or brothers bring them to Sunday school and those who have none canvass their neighbours for the privilege of bringing a visiting baby. Little girls carry in babies almost as big as themselves, staggering under their weight.

Babies with birthdays are especially popular, for then there is a ceremony in which the baby is taken to the Superintendent's desk, where he holds out a red and gold elephant with a slit in its back, into which the baby drops one penny for each year and "Happy Birthday" is sung by the school. Last Sunday a small five-year-old blonde in a pale pink velvet dress dropped in, with great dignity, ten pennies instead of five, for at the last minute she demanded the entire collection of her sponsors, under threat of not performing at all if she could not put in every copper in sight!

The people of St. Aidan's have not lived lives of ease. Some are out of work. Many have lost their securities. Death and sorrowing have come to them as it comes to all. The Memorial Tablet in the church bears names of sons, fathers and husbands. You see lamed men and shattered men in the congregations. But you hear no word of complaint. We have no soured old people or cynical young people.

They have something in this little church which causes them to walk in the light. If there are shadows, they fall behind them, not in front. The people have that priceless thing which Lloyd Douglas, in his "White Banners" calls *personal peace*. In the old Methodist Church, we used to call it an "experience of grace."

When one of the women of the congregation died this summer after a long and terrible illness, her husband, whose love and devotion had never wavered during these long years, was in his place at the door the next Sunday. He was haggard and greatly shaken but told us, with a radiant face, that she was sustained to the last. Angels had ministered to her and God in His mercy had dulled her pain so she could speak words of comfort to him before she fell asleep. She had fought a good fight, he said; she kept the faith!

"Have they any plan for bringing in the new social order?" a friend of mine asked me when I was telling her of our pleasant associations in the little church with these delightful people.

I could not say they had. Not a really definite, black and white plan, but they had a pattern—I know they have a pattern for their own lives that they try to follow. A pattern is more an individual and intimate thing than a plan, anyway; a warmer, closer experience; and so far as I can judge, their pattern is the one left to us long ago by a man called Micah and later confirmed and demonstrated by One who gave His life for it.

"He hath showed thee, Oh Man, what is good and what doth now the Lord require of thee? But to do justly, to love mercy and walk humbly with thy God."

^ Stained glass windows from St. Aidan's, donated by Premier Richard McBride.
ROBERT SMITH

"EVEN ON A SUNSHINY EXCURSION IT IS ALWAYS WELL TO HAVE A BOOK."

> 1936

A Tour of the Islands

Having two birthdays this week in our family, we felt we had to do something that could be remembered, so we picked up a few eatables, loaded the camera, left the garage door open for the martins who have a nest under the beam and drove to Swartz Bay, twenty-five miles north of Victoria, where the ferry *Cy Peck* was billed to leave at ten o'clock.

Cy Peck is a light little steamer, crisply white and black in its new coat of marine paint, and can carry 135 passengers when the occasion arises. Each day, except Wednesday, it makes four trips from Swartz Bay, which is a few miles north of Sidney, to Fulford Harbour on Salt Spring Island. But on Wednesday the little boat does a turn of the islands, giving an eight-hour excursion of changing delights.

There is Piers Island to see first, with its interesting and none-too-happy story of the incarceration of the Doukhobors for the offence of parading without clothing. For three years they were kept as prisoners on this island, men and women in separate compounds.

"Smarter fellows I never saw," said one of the ship's men, who had been a guard at the island for two years, and in proof of that he showed us a little tie-pin made by a Doukhobor. It is an ingenious little design, a bird with silver head, wings and tail and a coloured body. The material used for the body was the celluloid of a tooth-brush holder, with red and yellow paper below, taken from a nut bar. The silver came from an old teapot found on the island.

I asked about the women and how they spent their time. "They made drawn designs on the flour sacks," he said, "beautiful work, too. They would have done other work but they had nothing to do it with."

Evidently the government's objective in placing them on the island was punishment, not reform, for work was denied to these people to whom work is the dearest possession. The grim, bare buildings now stand gaunt and deserted and belong to the owners of the island.

Our first stop was at Fulford Harbour on Salt Spring Island, where the boat stayed two hours, giving us time to eat a leisurely lunch. We found, without difficulty, a little promontory where mossy stones made comfortable seats and where we could look across the estuary to the dim outline of the American shore. Before us on our left and right were the high hills running down to the sea, heavily wooded with evergreens and maples, the trees laid on like the plumage of a bird and showing a great variety of greens. Below us on the water-worn rocks the waves beat gently, for the day was still and the water rippled but slightly. Once in a while a ground swell rolled over in long undulations.

Nothing could be more peaceful or serene. We had shade under the trees, a view of the sea and mountains, not a mosquito or fly and the day was warm and pleasant, scented by the pine trees. There was even the friendly presence of a little black dog who joined our circle but politely declined to eat anything. His manner indicated that he did not wish to be misunderstood; his visit was purely social. We found out afterwards that the house above us belonged to the captain of the boat, so the little dog probably felt it was his duty to come down and welcome us in a semi-official capacity.

The boat, leaving Fulford Harbour, took us to Pender Island, Mayne and Galiano. At Mayne Island we stayed long enough to have tea at Grand View Lodge, run by Mrs. Naylor, in an old-fashioned dining room with point lace on the high shelf of the sideboard and pictures on the walls in carved wooden frames with leaves on the corners. We ate strawberry shortcake and drank tea out of nice old English china. We were served by a tall Swedish girl born in Hong Kong, the daughter of a missionary to the Chinese, who, we heard afterwards from one of Mrs. Naylor's boarders, is an accomplished pianist. She gave us folders advertising the beauties of Mayne Island in sincere but sketchy verse, from which I quote—

Why go to California to get a climate rare?
I'll let you in a secret, if you're looking for fresh air;
And when you've seen it through and through, I know you will
    exclaim:
There's nothing farther south to beat our Isle of Mayne.
There are stores upon the island and autos quite a lot,
With roads to take you all around and shade when you are hot…

In Mrs. Naylor's lawn there is a stump of a giant tree cut smoothly across to make a seat. We counted the rings of growth to tell its age and according to our record, it was three hundred years old. Some of the younger members of the party discovered dry seasons and periods of high winds and deep snow, but we had to leave them at that point.

It was on the veranda at Mrs. Naylor's that we saw a bulletin of the church services of Galiano, Mayne Island, Port Washington, Saturna and North Galiano. The services were divided quite evenly between the first four, but North Galiano seems to be cut pretty short. It gets a service at 11:00 a.m. on each fifth Sunday, which will be four each year with a possible five on leap year.

The Gulf Islands are many in number and have a population of about three thousand people, a third of which are residents of Salt Spring. Many of [the islands] are merely reefs where a few brave trees hang perilously to the rocks.

The first settlers came in row-boats sixty years ago, took up land on larger islands, cleared away the forest, set out orchards and gardens, fished in the winter time and made a living, without anyone's help. Now there are farms on the islands being worked by the third generation, still happy contented people. There are very few people receiving relief on the islands. Poultry, dairying, seed raising, gardening and fruit farming are the common industries, and of late years the tourist trade gives occupation to many. Galiano last year had 850 people from outside.

They claim that their climate is better than that of Victoria and can prove that they have more rain and less wind. Whatever it is they have, it suits them, and a more contented people cannot be found anywhere. One woman who came on the boat boasts that she has not been away from Salt Spring Island for twelve years and expressed surprise that anyone should think this remarkable. "Why should I leave?" she said. "We have everything here. We have boats calling regularly; we get the papers from Victoria and Vancouver, we have sunsets, tennis courts, dramatic club, churches, neighbours, radio. What more do we want?" And there could be no answer to that.

One man on the boat, who has lived on one of the islands for many years, said to me that he looks for a great many people to come in during the next few years. People can live so well on such a small income, he said. I asked him what he meant by a small income and he said $600 a year, and that, he said, would provide an abundant living for a family. He also told me that the peace and security of the islands attracts people from the south who are frightened by the kidnapping of recent years [referring to the Lindbergh baby kidnapping of 1932] and mentioned a peninsula on Salt Spring Island on which an American woman was building a beautiful home.

When we left Mayne Island and headed for home through Active Pass we had a feeling that the picnic was drawing to a close. The lunch had been eaten at Fulford Harbour and at Mayne Island we had tea. We had watched the young people skipping on the lower deck and talked to every one who would talk. I went upstairs and began to read *Mary Peters* again. Even on a sunshiny excursion it is always well to have a book. Suddenly I heard people on the deck taking excitedly and I hurried out.

A school of black fish was on the left, blowing and tumbling, black fins showing like little tents on the water; so many we could not watch them all. We knew the other fish would have their hearts in their mouths when these hungry and roomy monsters were after them, for they were the black fish or killer whales, the terror of the sea.

Many of the passengers had seen them before but not so close. I had seen them only in pictures.

Suddenly we saw some of them ahead of the boat rolling, turning, blowing sprays of water into the air; and as they rolled there was sometimes a gleam of white, which puzzled those of our number who knew something of whales. I heard about them from one of the passengers. Whales are not fish; they are mammals just as much as cows or sheep, and they have to come up to the surface of the water to breathe, and their tails are not set on like fish tails but horizontally, to make it easier to rise in the water. The blowing occurs when they come up and clear out the water from their lungs before taking a breath.

While I was listening to this, the whales were in front of us and suddenly began a series of leaps into the air; they hooped themselves and sprang clear out of the water, a dazzling display of black and white. We could see the flukes in their tails and the big triangular fins. There were three of them in the performing group, one of which remained until it seemed that the boat might hit him.

We hurried to the back of the boat then and watched the performance until the boat had gone too far for us to see them. The friend who had been telling me about them said he had never seen them leaping like this, nor did he know that they had so much white on them. The second mate explained the presence of the whales by a proprietary wave of his hand: "We've arranged with them for Wednesday performances all season," he said.

I heard of another great monster seen in these waters two months ago, a tiger shark, forty feet long with black stripes around his gills. He had, no doubt, drifted north from the tropical waters of the south and when seen was in a state of languor, probably caused by the colder water or the lack of proper food.

I have not said half enough about the scenery, for in addition to the wild natural beauty of sea and mountains there are glimpses of the gardens, cultivated fields with plants in even rows; the presence of fat cattle lying in the shade of spreading trees; the dignified little weather-beaten churches; beautiful homes set in protecting shrubberies as if their owners wished to think their own thoughts, undisturbed even by the presence of a passing boat; the activities of the little ports of call; and the endless change of scene as the boat winds and turns through the aisles of the sea; heralding its approach by a deep-throated whistle that tears the echoes from the mountain sides.

Eight hours of this, on a day of clear sunshine, warm and pine-scented, leaves a memory of complete tranquility and an added sense of the diversity and richness of the Canadian scene.

"CHRISTMAS IS A POOR TIME
TO KEEP A GOOD COOK IN JAIL."

A Christmas Story

I would not have chosen an unemployment camp for the setting of a Christmas story. I have always thought of them as dull houses of frustrated hopes where young hearts grow sad and bitter and life loses all dimensions but that of length. But it is quite possible that none of us knows the full magic of Christmas and how it works its way, even into sombre places.

This is the story of Mack, the cook at one of the camps on the Coast, and Mack was no ordinary camp cook. Mack had a knack [for] putting food together. He had a gift. It was Mack who discovered that prunes soaked in warm water until they have lost all their wrinkles could be cooked in the pan beside a roast of pork, imparting a flavour to the pork that made even the superintendent come out to the kitchen and ask him how it came about. It was Mack who raised green peppers from seed in a sunny place that he had dug and cared for, and cooked them with rice and tomatoes and cheese and salt pork and breadcrumbs, making every fellow his friend for life.

Mack had the gift! And you would never think it to look at him,

53

for he was a thin, pale little fellow, with a child's voice and a bare face that never needed shaving.

Soon after he came to the camp, he got in right, one time when the bread ran out, by whipping up some sour milk biscuits and sprinkling cinnamon on them when he put them in the oven. The superintendent again made comment and at the end of three months Mack was installed as head cook and allowed to pick his own assistants. It was the fact of Mack's cooking that started the Christmas fund. About the end of November, the boys began talking of Christmas dinners they had had in happier seasons when they had jobs or were going to school and living at home. And someone made the statement that there was no one who could put up a better Christmas dinner than Mack "if he had the groceries." So the fund began. Twenty cents a day is not a lavish wage, but out of it twenty-two dollars was raised to buy whatever Mack thought he should have. And Mack was deputed to go to town and make the purchases. It was to be Mack's one holiday, too, so the superintendent told him to stay the day.

Mack had saved seven dollars of his own and he knew what he was going to do with it. Mack had his plans—one luxury and one only would he allow himself. He hired a car for the afternoon. He wanted to feel again a steering wheel in his hand. But first he did his shopping. He spent the camp money as cautiously as any MacTavish ever did. He consulted with the head of the grocery department of one of the big stores and got every advantage of bargain prices, past or future, on his turkeys. By buying his turkeys at the big store his purchases would be delivered free of charge. He spent the whole morning in and out of bargain basements assembling all his purchases at last and having them delivered with the turkeys. Methodically he checked his list and saved all his bills. At the end he had four cents on hand but had bought everything.

When the business of the day was over, Mack gave himself the luxury of eating what someone else had cooked. And then began his holiday, which was a drive around town. At ten o'clock at night he was still driving. He had been around Marine Drive twice, out to the Butchart Gardens and up the Island highway. Now even the business streets of Victoria are swept and clear of traffic at this hour, as we all know, and as Mack viewed the clear length of Yates Street with its beautiful lights like clusters of white grapes, a sudden desire for speed swept his careful soul! It might be a whole year before he had another holiday and when would he ever have his hands on a car? Just one grand burst of speed before he took the car back! There was not a soul in sight.

At the corner of Quadra, the Law on a motorcycle drew up beside him and he slowed down; all the weight that had been in his foot was now in his heart.

"Where are you going, Doctor?" said the hardest voice he had ever heard.

In spite of Mack's tearful pleadings, the Law was adamant. Speeding must cease. There had been accidents. Orders had been issued to gather all offenders. Too bad—but he should have thought about all this about ten seconds before he stepped on the gas! "Twenty-five dollars or ten days."

Mack begged for a postcard and painfully inscribed it to the superintendent. Words were so feeble, and so hard to come by—

Dear Sir:
I'm in jail for speeding, but I got the stuff O.K.
Merry Christmas to all, I'm sorry.
Mack

The next night the camp was in a state of panic. No Mack and no groceries, for the stores make deliveries only twice a week. Had he gone with their money? Were they to be cheated out of their Christmas dinner after all? If Mack had fooled them, whom could you trust? The murmurings grew into a clamour. The superintendent was firm in his opinion that Mack had not absconded. It was he who thought of jail as a possible explanation, but advised patience. Give him another day, or two days. Meanwhile the new cook was having trouble. He was lost without his chief and everyone's temper was touchy. Nothing he could do pleased the "boarders." He burned the porridge and cooked potatoes with a bone in them, and mutiny seemed certain.

On the third day, Mack's card came, also the turkeys and groceries, which were unpacked and put in the storage kitchen by the disconsolate cook, who knew the cooking of these was far beyond him. If he spoiled them, nothing would save him.

That day a delegation went to the superintendent's office—two men, with the cook between them. They had a proposition to make. The superintendent listened attentively. "We got to get Mack out of jail," the spokesman said. "This man," eyeing the downcast Pete with disapproval, "can't boil water without burning it. Now the turkeys and everything are here, we just feel we must get Mack to come back. Would you take Pete here into town and turn him over to the Magistrate—he ought to be in jail anyway for the things he had done—and let him work out Mack's sentence, whatever it is?"

"What have you to say to this, Peter?" the superintendent asked. "Are you willing to go to jail?"

"Glad to go anywhere," he answered, "to get away from this gang. Nothing pleases them. I've worked my fingers to the bone for them and what do I get? Sure I'll go to jail and like the company. It will be a swell change for me."

The superintendent drove into Victoria that day, taking Pete with him for safe-keeping and went to the Magistrate, explaining the situation. He told about the twenty-two dollars and the turkeys—and dwelt on Mack's great skill as a cook and the strained situation at the camp under Pete's cooking, with Christmas only two days away. He described the delegation and Pete's willingness to take Mack's place. Might he ask for Mack's release?

"On what grounds?" the Magistrate asked. "He was driving fifty—and had no excuse and made to plea—he wasn't drunk."

"No, he wouldn't be," the superintendent pleaded, "but don't you see, your Honour, he hasn't had his hand on a car for a year and I suppose it went to his head a bit. He forgot just for a moment that he was definitely out of work, and he didn't hurt anyone. Besides, we need him at the camp—I really can't do without him."

The Magistrate hesitated. It was irregular. Still—it did seem too bad to disappoint the whole camp, and these camps are difficult places at best—Christmas is a poor time to keep a good cook in jail. He began writing on the desk pad. The superintendent followed his hand and read, "Released on grounds of compassion." Then, looking up, he said with a smile, "In consideration of this season of goodwill, we will grant your request and we will not insist on the sentence being completed by the gentleman known as Pete. He, too, is entitled to a merry Christmas, even if he did burn the porridge, and let me wish you both the compliments of the season."

After Mack had a shave and a haircut, he and the superintendent did some more shopping for the party. When they arrived at the camp, the full force was waiting for them and received them with cheers. They even forgave Pete his evil workings, now that they knew the food was safe from his blundering hands.

All that day Mack worked and all through the night. He peeled apples, chopped meat and suet for the mince pies. Pete assisted by scraping vegetables, keeping fires on, carrying water, grating the bread for the dressing and peeling the onions. The turkeys were cooked with strips of bacon laid across the breasts and sausages under the wings—many sausages to make the meat go further. Mack had thought of everything, even to the little whirls of white tissue paper to cover the ends of the drumsticks. For a centrepiece on the table, he had a little log cabin made of peeled withes, which one of the men sat up late to finish, and a rail fence around it made of candy sticks. The roof of the cabin lifted off and inside it was filled with homemade candy, made by Mack at three o'clock on Christmas morning. The table had long strips of red tissue paper on the white oilcloth and the turkeys were brought in on their big platters, sending out their delicious odour of sage and onions—blue enamel dishes of cranberries were dotted up and down the table. Giblet-gravy and open dishes of mashed potatoes, mashed turnips, creamed carrots and pickled beets completed the setting. When everyone at the camp sat down together, staff and men, the superintendent at the head of the table, every face wore a smile and every man wished his neighbour a "Merry Christmas."

"NOT A SOUL DID I KNOW, BUT I KNEW I WAS ON THE RIGHT BOAT BY THE CONVERSATION."

> APRIL 24, 1937

I began to feel at home as soon as I walked up the gangplank of the Victoria boat, ducked my head under the red flag, checked my hand baggage and then came up the stairs to the lounge. The wicker chairs, with the hollow seats and footstools, gave me a welcome and I sat down in one that had a cushion and looked around me.

Not a soul did I know, but I knew I was on the right boat by the conversation. "I intended to stay longer, but, my dear, it is so noisy." "I heard from Avery that the camellia is in bloom and so I had to come." "They are always rushing about ... really it grows more like an American city every day ... I longed for our own quiet place by the sea."

... Being a holiday weekend, the boat was full of children, beautiful children, well dressed and exemplary in manners. A lovely little girl of eight led her brother to a seat near me. I could see he was a care, but her face was marked by high resolve. She had probably prayed for a brother and was going to abide by the bargain. Later, the younger brother, bursting from her discipline, stumbled over my feet and returned, at his sister's instigation, to apologize.

"I am sorry, I am very ashamed," he said, all in one breath. I wanted to kiss him, but I knew that would be a fatal blunder, so

I accepted his apology gravely and silently hoped he would do it again. Indeed I was ready to have my corn stepped on if it would bring him back.

The day was one of the bright, warm days when the five hours go by like a flash. The sea sparkled, the gulls circled, the boat cut the water proudly and all the sordid worrying things of life fell away from us, as flimsy and fleeting as the foam behind the boat!

When we were just one hour from Victoria, we passed Gordon Head and I tried to show a nurse from Winnipeg, with whom I was sitting, the exact location of the Lantern Lane house. There it was, looking about the size of a child's block, beyond Walter Paterson's pasture and just north of Stewart Skilling's fine crown of trees. The red roof could be distinguished and that was all.

I found it hard to get much response even from my good friend the nurse. There was not much to see, to be sure. It was something like showing the baby's first tooth to a family friend.

I tried to tell her how interesting the drive from Victoria is and especially the long straight stretch of Shelbourne Street with the booth where puppies are sold in the open. Poor little fellows, with their big, sad eyes, placed there to sell themselves to the careless passerby, and how dangerous it is, if you do not want one, to stop for even a look. The sign reads: "Puppies for sale, Kittens free." So if the puppies suffer an indignity by being offered for sale on a public highway, what about the kittens, set out "with no par value"?

And now I have been at home for two days and I have been around to see how the plants wintered. The forsythia is a mass of golden blossoms and the low daphne bush is in bloom, with its perfect little pale purple flowerets, heavy with perfume. The peach trees behind the garage have had a hard pruning and are fastened firmly to the wall. Hitherto they grew as they liked and ran to wood and leaves, but now they are full of blossoms under the new discipline. The peach tree on the south wall of the house is in blossom, too, and when we are washing dishes at the sink we look at its pink blossoms and forget to work.

A man is plowing a field, with the gulls following him by the hundred, dropping on the new furrows in search of worms. He told me last year that once he plowed down a gull and did not notice it until he had come back and there it was, completely submerged, all but a tip of one wing. But it was not the worse when he released it. Gulls have a stout heart.

Far be it from me to interject a sad note in the joyous atmosphere of homecoming. I realize it is no time to be telling of agricultural pests, aphids, blight, tent caterpillars, or the like. In fact, these are all quiescent at the time and invisible, and it is well to let sleeping dogs lie.

But here is one garden destroyer that has had its way during my absence and I will explain its method of operation. When you plant seed in the autumn, putting stakes around the planting, with name of plant on same, at intervals, and feel you have made this corner of the earth safe from *Physalis franchetti*, which is to say, Japanese Lanterns; and when you return to the scene of your endeavours, months later, expecting to find the tiny plants nosing up from the earth and find instead the soil freshly cultivated and trenched for some other planting and all evidence destroyed, you know it has fallen a victim to the hoe-worm, and there is not much you can do about it. At least there is not much I can do. I married one!

"BUT NOTHING SPOILED THE SUNSHINE OF YESTERDAY."

took a day off yesterday.

It was the yellow morning sunshine coming in through the window where I sat reading the paper that suggested the idea. The sunlight was warm and comforting, and made a pool of glory on the floor, and as I sat there I wanted time to stand still. It could never be sweeter than this.

Every cloud in the sky had marched away, leaving a perfect blue bowl over our heads. The windows were open to air the house after the damp, cold weather, when all the fires had been kept going. So the fresh air was welcome.

As it billowed the curtains, I could see they were dusty, but even that did not rouse me. What difference did it make? What difference did anything make on a morning like this?

I went outside to get the real tang of the air and to hear the skylarks. They were full of song, these enchanted singers that lead a charmed life. How they escape the cats and crows I cannot tell, for they do not even seek the safety of the trees, but nest on the ground under strawberry stalks, or any little shelter, and somehow survive. They are so precious and dear and small. Each spring their song comes like another assurance of God's continued care.

61

This day was all the brighter because we have had snow, deep enough to put all the birds on the bread line. A speaker over the radio the day it snowed appealed for the little people, dependent now on human charity. I am sure there was a ready response.

We have a garden table were the bread is spread, and on the snowy day two gulls came, but something held them back. I watched them through the window as they made several attempts to move in on the little birds. But when one advanced toward the table, the other beat him back. At last they fought it out and flew away, full of recriminations, and the juncos and robins were left in peace.

The snow, which came after the cold weather, saved the bulbs from injury by drawing the frost. Nothing seems to be hurt. The yellow crocuses make fairy rings under the monkey trees.

We brought some of the blossoms into the house and put them in water to see them open wide and fold up again at night. The next day the water had turned yellow, and I put a piece of white cotton in to see if it would take the dye. I could see in this a new dye called "Crocus Yellow."

I have often done this with Indian paintbrush, which colours the water pink and from this gets its name. All went well until the tiny members of the family decided this glass of crocuses had been in the house long enough. So my scientific research ended.

But nothing spoiled the sunshine of yesterday. The Olympics, blue and white, smiled down on us. Mount Baker, over the shoulder of San Juan Island, looked more and more like a partly melted dish of ice cream. Haro Strait, between us and San Juan, dimpled and rippled.

The fields steamed in the warm air, and I am sure every bulb felt a stirring in its little heart. Fat robins stepped about the lawn intent on the extraction of worms from the grass. Catkins are hanging from the nut trees. Every year they promise nuts, but none have come so far. But I believe them again this year.

The little holly trees are shining in their tightly set leaves. Someday they will grow into a full hedge, with red berries in the fall and winter. We have 80 of them in a row, grown from seed. The birds carry the berries from the holly farm nearby, and so in the woods come the hardy seedlings, growing by their own free will. When you see one growing, you know it has passed the elimination test; the weak ones have died.

One of the neighbours came out on the early bus to enjoy the sunshine with me, and strangely enough we talked of cold weather and the ways we contrived to keep warm when winter storms raged on the prairie.

We spoke of taking hot stove-lids wrapped in newspapers to bed and recalled the smell of the almost singeing paper. We remembered that the "bridge" of the stove was in special favour, because it could seldom be spared. Pots could be placed on the stove holes, but the "bridge" had no substitute unless the boiler was pressed into service.

A black iron pot filled with coals was often used to take the chill off the room. But its hours were numbered and in the morning it seemed to add to the cold. We recalled the tub full of water that sat in the cellar to keep the potatoes and apples from freezing, and the newspapers next to the glass in the windows to preserve the precious flowers.

All this was far enough away to be pleasant to remember. And it brought back a time when life held no outside fears. The world was safe, even if the winters were cold in Manitoba. Queen Victoria was on the throne, and the "open Bible was the secret of England's greatness."

We did not know much about governments and their ways. They did not concern us. We were not looking for any help. What we did not have we did without, and everyone knew that prosperity was ahead.

The man who was willing to work was sure to succeed. We learned that from the copy-books; also from observation.

So we endured patiently, knowing summer would come, crops would grow, prices would go up and the next year would be the best one yet.

I walked down the lane with my friend when she went away. We knew exactly when to leave the house, for Jimmie, the driver, is never late. Round the bend and up the hill came the orange coach that serves the travelling needs of Gordon Head. (When we think Jimmie is late, we know our watches are wrong.)

Ferndale Road lay silent and empty, quivering with sunshine after the bus went by. I stayed to look at the purple aubrieta, which grows outside the fence. The neighbourhood never looked lovelier, for I was saying goodbye to it again. Blooms will come and fall before I shall see it again. But I put that thought away as unworthy of such a day.

ii. Foreshadows of War

Nellie McClung's columns *appeared at a time when the country, and much of the world, was still in the dry, dirty clutches of the Great Depression. Overseas, fascism was on the rise, and Europe was bracing itself for another war. Nellie, ensconced at Lantern Lane with its idyllic garden and charming neighbours, could have easily ignored the global turmoil, but this was not in her character. Although she was in her sixties and in poor health, Nellie still made every effort to meet her obligations, even though she wondered at times if her actions were driven more by ego than by altruism.*

In 1936, Nellie was the only woman to be appointed to the board of governors of the newly formed Canadian Broadcasting Corporation; she served on the board until 1942. She was also the only female member of the Canadian delegation to the League of Nations between 1936 and 1938 (though Charlotte Witton had served before her). These obligations gave her the opportunity to travel, both across the country and overseas, and theoretically gave her a stronger platform from which to promote women's voices and rights. However, Nellie—who was a grassroots activist at heart—quickly grew disappointed with both organizations. *The male directors of the CBC determined that women's voices were too shrill to be broadcast over the radio and defeated Nellie's efforts to keep liquor advertising off the airwaves. The League of Nations was not the effective vehicle of peace and progress that it had set out to be, and Nellie likely wished she had heeded the warning of friend and former delegate Charlotte Whitton, who warned Nellie that she should prepare to be "sickeningly disillusioned" by the international body.*

Despite the tumultuous state of the world and the number of miles Nellie travelled on official business, her columns in the years leading up to the war strike a balance between matters of international importance and those of domestic—very domestic—interest. On more than one occasion, Nellie writes about the encroaching forces of death and destruction overseas in one paragraph and the state of her garden in the next. This might have been her own style choice, but there is some indication that her editor was pressuring her to be more folksy than strident in her columns. She begins one column by urging "Mr. Editor" not to be upset that her piece for the week was not intended as political commentary. In reality, though, political and social matters were never far from Nellie's mind, and even when she talks at length about red ants or onion growing or the hardiness of kale, she is almost always making a statement about something greater.

Nellie travelled widely during this period, but her travels were rarely the focus of her columns. Perhaps she was aware that her readers did not have the privilege of seeing the world as she did, and thus she sought to connect with them by focusing on the joys of returning home. And although "home" for Nellie was now Lantern Lane on Vancouver Island, her love for the Canadian Prairies and her deep sense of kinship with the prairie people were never far from her heart. As the following columns show, Nellie was an expert at speaking to ordinary people across western Canada and beyond about the issues that mattered to them.

"IT IS WELL TO GIVE PRESENTS THAT CAUSE ACTIVITY."

> DECEMBER 1937

This matter of giving is on our minds, now that December has come in.

In August, I am sure that in my Christmas giving I will not squander much money on Christmas cards. In August, I am sure that the money spent on Christmas cards has been unwisely spent. But when December comes driving in with slanting spears of sleet, when the days are short, and the nights are long, and the wind mourns in the chimney, and the trees are all bare and the landscape desolate, I want all the bells and candles and Christmas trees and stars and tinsel I can get and I want to buy cards in boxes and look them over carefully and send them far and wide, with something written on every one of them.

I like fireside scenes with a cat on the homemade mat, and I like stockings hung beside the fire and a kettle hung from a black hook above the flames, and I like coaching scenes and people walking along snowy streets with their arms full of parcels and horse-drawn sleighs full of happy people, and I like, too, scenes of village churches where the people are flocking in to sing "O Holy Night" and "O Little Town of Bethlehem."

The price of a gift bears but little relation to its value. Some inexpensive things are able to defy the attrition of time. I remember the first time I left home, aged sixteen, going out to teach in a country school in Manitoba. The neighbours gathered the night before and presented me with gifts beautiful and welcome: two pairs of stockings from Mrs. Merrell, handkerchiefs from Mrs. Naismith, plaid silk for a blouse from my sister Lizzie, and a motto from Mrs. Ingram.

The stockings ran their course; the handkerchiefs are no more; even the plaid blouse came and went, but it is not as completely gone as the others, for I have a picture of it, with myself in it. But the motto, though corporeally it has no doubt long since returned to the dust from which it came, still lives in my memory. I hung it on the wall of the school and often drew comfort from it when the long afternoon was closing. The lines could never be classified as poetry, but they carried a message even as a piece of brown paper may wrap a jewel:

> *Do not look at life's long sorrow,*
> *See how small each moment's pain;*
> *God will help you on the morrow,*
> *So each day begins again.*

At that gathering of friends to which I have just referred, when I was about to leave the friendly shelter of the old house on the farm, my brother Will contributed a whole set of Dickens, and it was from these volumes that I first became conscious of what literature can mean, and having received that early, it went deep. I was able to look into other days and see the shaping of human destiny.

Christmas is a time for friendly giving and experimental giving, thoughtfully carried out. It is well to give presents that cause activity. The present that only pleases for the first few minutes is a poor one. When the Women's Institute in a certain prairie village gave presents to three old ladies, their first thought was to give a bed jacket and hot water bottle to each one. But fortunately the president was a woman of vision.

"Don't do it," she said. "Old ladies, like our three, do not want to be reminded of their rheumatism and the fact that they are likely to remain more and more in bed. Let us buy them the wool and give each of them a different Afghan book, so that a competition will be held."

Christmas giving should have in it that essence of hospitality that binds the elements of a nation together. Let us never forget the Family who found no room at the Inn. Let us do one thing at least to make some stranger feel the impact of kindliness.

"AND SHE WOULD KNOW WHAT
THE LARKS WERE SINGING ABOUT."

When William White, at work in his garden, heard his wife calling him in, he dropped his hoe and went in, making some excuse to his daughters for his appearance. He couldn't very well tell them their mother had called him, for their mother had been dead and buried for a week.

But he could not ignore the call, either. No one ever called him "William" in just that tone and he couldn't let Minnie call in vain, no matter what the girls thought. After all, Minnie meant more to him than anyone. Dead or alive, Minnie had the first claim on him. It was "William" she called for when the pain was heaviest on her. She often said he was better than any doctor. And "William" was the last word on her lips. She seemed to know when he was sitting beside her in the hospital, and after she could no longer speak he thought he felt a little pressure in her hand. So he stayed every night until the nurses put him out. Not exactly that, but they had a way of bustling around, getting ready for the night and letting him know he should go.

And when the end came, she suddenly looked strong again and well and even young and her hand closed on his. He knew what she meant. It was Minnie's way of telling him she was just going on ahead and she wouldn't forget. Of course, he couldn't tell that to

71

anyone. They would think he was just an old man gone queer after his wife died.

People thought it was odd to see the old man so composed at the funeral. The girls hung around him tenderly, saying, "Now, father, you must be brave; remember she is better off."

He took it all without protest, but William White knew better. Minnie had not wanted to leave him. She didn't want to be better off. He and Minnie had talked about it many times and he remembered what she said. So when he heard her calling, he always came, because she just might be back. Some people are gone when they're dead. You know they are gone. But Minnie was different. Even the grave couldn't blot out Minnie.

The spring came in the old man's garden. Spring had always been an adventure to them. The grape hyacinths and crocuses were out and the buds were getting bigger on the cherry trees and the larks singing high in the air, so full of joy.

Just then he saw the minister driving into the yard and a feeling of impatience came over him. Not that he did not like Mr. Peters. No one could have spoken more beautifully the day of the funeral. But he wanted to get on with the digging. She had bought a lot of new bulbs that fall that he must get in. She always liked to have all the bulbs in by Easter. Well, he'd go on until he was called. Elizabeth would soon be out after him. She would be glad of an excuse to get him away from his work—always nagging at him not to get overheated, telling him he was not as young as he used to be and he must be careful.

He went on digging as hard as he could, with a real enjoyment in every stroke. The ground now, the soil, the good earth, had comfort in it. Mother Earth! No wonder we call it Mother Earth. God's good gift to man. Minnie had often said she had no dread of it. It would lie easy on her and she knew she would hear the music of the rain above her head and the song of the grass growing and the larks. And she would know what the larks were singing about.

Just then he saw the Millers and the Stevens drive in the gate and he knew he would have to go in. Too bad they had to come on a nice day like this, when he was feeling so strong and keen at his work. Elizabeth would be all apologies because he was not dressed. Usually she hailed him in at three o'clock, for the neighbours had been good to drop in since Minnie went, thinking he was lonesome. He'd go on digging as long as he could.

They could have their visit with each other. The spade seemed to lift the earth itself. Suddenly he heard her call, strong and clear!

Dropping his spade, he turned and saw her. She came down the path with all her old energy and radiance.

"You're young, Minnie," he cried in surprise. "How does it come you're so young?" He knew then that he had never doubted she would come!

Minnie laughed and kissed him. "You're young yourself, William," she said, looking at him with her eyes sparkling.

They stood together under the cherry tree they had planted the first year they were married—the cherry tree on which the buds were breaking.

"Will you stay with me, Minnie?" he asked at last. "I know you will if you can, but can you stay?"

Her hand tightened on his, a young hand, firm and warm. "You will come with me," she said. "We'll never part now, William. It's all true—all that the larks tried to tell us. The neighbours are all here. The front of the house is full of the saddest people you ever saw, all the neighbours. They think you are dead, William, just as they thought I was dead a month ago. Listen, William, and we can hear them. Mr. Peters is reading. Lovely words, great promises, clear as sunshine, but they only hope they are true. They would not look like that if they believed them."

The words came through the open windows.

"Let not your heart be troubled. I am the resurrected and the life! If any man believe in Me, he shall never die! For we know if this earthly tabernacle be dissolved, we have a building of God, a house not made with hand, eternal in the Heavens!"

But the people who looked out of the windows saw nothing but an old man's garden, full of sunshine, cherry trees coming into bloom, and a spade still stuck in the ground, just as he left it, the day he was called.

73

"THE TIMES ARE BRITTLE."

I envy the people who see only one side of any question. It saves so much mental wear and tear, and gives a serenity of soul and a poise that we all crave. It requires special mental attributes, of course. Lack of imagination will help and a comfortable ingredient of complacency with traces of dumbness. A large family connection also seems to be a favourable environment for this type of mind. To be able to buttress the individual opinion with the seasoned judgment of Uncle James gives it a measure of documentary authority.

I am thinking about it now, for on my recent journey to Ottawa I have had numerous conversations with people. Naturally we spoke of the European situation. I talked with two people, a man and a woman, who know exactly what should be done. Neither of them has a doubt.

They believe that Great Britain has been the guardian angel of the world and has the sanction of heaven on all her ways. The man believes that war is a holy thing and by it great things have been achieved. He believes all soldiers are beloved of God, and "he who dies fighting hath increase."

Before I left him, though, I asked if German and Japanese soldiers are included.

"Certainly not," he said, "for they are no better than slaves; theirs are the selfish and arrogant countries. In fact, they are 'the enemy on who destruction will fall.'"

"Have you never read history?" he asked.

The woman, whom I met later, told me prophecy was being fulfilled before our eyes. I expressed the hope that war would be averted. She said Great Britain will have to meet her enemies, but there is nothing to fear. She will overcome them all. It is written in the pyramids!

The common quality in these two people is that they are sure of something. They see their own country victorious, if war should come, and that leads one to ponder on what is victory in war.

At the end of the last war, the Allies certainly were victorious. Germany lay at their feet, beaten and broken. So they laid on her debt for reparations that she could never pay. They demanded of her more gold than there was in all the world. Millions of young men lay dead, others were blind, maimed and broken; hearts were sad and bitter all over the world. What good is there in victory? And what permanence? So long as hatreds remain, war will come again and again.

No race will live at peace with the world under a sense of injustice. The only way that war could settle anything would be by ruthless extermination of the enemy. Not even my military enthusiasts would go that far.

Here are some facts which are inescapable: Six countries, including Great Britain, France and Russia, control three-quarters of the Earth's surface, leaving the other quarter for the sixty-eight other countries, including Germany, Italy and Japan. The same six countries own eighty-five per cent of all the raw materials in the world, leaving fifteen per cent for the other sixty-eight. It is not reasonable to think that this state of affairs will last forever.

Long before Adolf Hitler appeared on the scene, a German chancellor, Dr. Stresemann, said to a representative of the British Foreign Office: "If you could have given me some concession, I could have won this generation of Germans for peace. That you could not—or would not—has been my tragedy—and your crime."

It may be too late, but who knows that? Prime Minister Chamberlain sees it. He has been thoroughly abused and reviled, but the historian of the future will see that he really prevented the outbreak of war by his gesture of appeasement.

To gain a few weeks, a few days even, is something. The times are brittle. Anything can happen. And yet we know the Spirit of God has not ceased to arrive with men. He did not make the world and then withdraw to let us fight it out among ourselves.

There are so many evidences of God's presence, so many lovely things circling us around. Civilization is worth saving. It is worth fighting for, if we could be sure we can save it that way. If we could be sure that bloodletting would bring peace, plenty, prosperity, goodwill, contentment and beauty to everyone, there are many who would sign on in that great campaign.

But it has been tried. The battlefields of the world have been watered by clean, young blood, the best we had, and yet the crop that grew was a poisonous crop. We are reaping it now.

It would seem to be the part of wisdom to try another method, a way of self-sacrifice, too, remembering the combined promise and warning given long ago that "he who seeketh to save his life shall lose it, and he who is willing to lose his life shall save it." Let us see if that can be applied to nations.

A new World Conference could be called, laying aside all national pride, by the six nations who hold the 75 percent of the Earth and 85 percent of its raw materials, inviting others to join and assuring them of concessions. It would be a costly conference, but not so costly as a war, and its object would be peace.

There would have to be a new spirit of turning the cheek. All of which requires more courage than to march off to war, with drums beating and the fife pealing and with hearts made fiery by hatred. It will all depend on how much we want peace and how much we are willing to pay for peace.

Are we like Artemus Ward, who said he was such a lover of peace he was willing to sacrifice every last one of his wife's relations?

As a matter of fact, a re-arranged world might not cause anyone any great distress. There really is enough for everyone. Australia might have to give up her dream of an all-white country. (It is always wise to make the definite application as far away from home as possible.)

I will not mention what Canada might have to do. This is no time for argument.

I wonder how many of us would be willing to accept a lower standard of living, if by doing so we could bring peace and security to all the world. Let us have a show of hands.

"ANTS SEEM TO BE THE ONLY INSECTS WHO KEEP
SLAVES AND MAKE OTHER INSECTS DO THEIR BIDDING."

> JUNE 28, 1938

The shadows of the big trees down the road are black on the grass and the daffodil stalks are withering in the hot afternoon sunshine.

A forest fire on San Juan Island has filled the gulf with smoke, and the white rabbit's head (which is the top of Mount Baker) has turned to a murky pink. I know a place where every bit of breeze will come, under a cherry tree on the lawn, but the whole neighbourhood is so full of industry that I feel I must work, even if it is the hottest day we have had this year.

When I listen I hear hoes and cultivators and there is a sound of water running, for all the hoses are going at full force. The one I can see is throwing a lazy lash of water on the bed that will receive the eggplants tomorrow. The eggplants have been growing in a greenhouse and are now about four inches high and ready to plant out.

The martins are taking mouthfuls of mud from the puddle beside one of the taps, to build their nests. A fat robin is having a bath in the earthen basin that stands above a rockery; a quail in a tree is calling "cut-that-out" to the world at large.

Everywhere I look, I see somebody at work, so instead of seeking the cool spot under the cherry tree, I go out to have another look at our anthill. Maybe they will inspire me to do something.

We have an anthill of our own. Red ants, too. They were here when we came and have been increasing each year. We always give our visitors an invitation to come to see the ants. If they are interested in this small colony, we offer to show them the Greater New York Colony, down in the woods.

The big settlement has been many years in building and has radial highways leading away from it. Some ruthless person cut a hole in the big dome with a spade once, just to see what would happen, and the ants built it up in a few weeks. No doubt they measure time by this catastrophe, as the Regina people still speak of the cyclone and Victoria of the Deep Snow.

In our own small colony there is great activity with pieces of straw and dead cherry blossoms. The workers are carrying them in; some pushing, some pulling; and it is hard to tell what they are trying to do. They seem to be getting in each other's way and hindering each other, with no one to direct the traffic. But I suppose an upper view of one of our busy streets would leave an observer confused, too.

I keep trying to find out who are the overseers. In Mexico, on the roads, it was easy to tell the "boss" man. In every seven men, one does nothing but see that the other six work. But among the ants everyone is active and there seems to be no plan at all. Solomon was no doubt correct when he said they had no guide or overseer and yet gather their meat in the summer.

I find that ants have a literature of their own. Literally hundreds of books have been written about them. Maeterlinck says they are the aristocrats of the insect world, giving them even a higher place than bees. Ants seem to be the only insects who keep slaves and make other insects do their bidding.

The green flies are their cows, yielding them part of their food in the form of honeydew, which the ants extract from them. When a rose bush is sprayed with Black Leaf 40, the ants rush in and carry away the green flies to a place of safety. Naturally, the owner will save his cow if he can.

In some communities the ants make enclosures for their cattle, building a roof over them and an underground passage to make it easy for them to go in and out in all weathers.

The ants' colony is a matriarchate where love rules, and the love is not love for each other but for the race. Maeterlinck, in his book *The Life of the Ant*, says that nowhere in nature can be found so magnificent a maternal love.

The hen will defend her chickens against an enemy but she does not know the value of her eggs. But an ant loves the larvae, for to her it represents the future. An ant knows no fear when the larva is in danger.

The centre of gravity of conscience and happiness is not where it is with us. We give our first love to ourselves and our own family. The ant cares nothing for herself. If a fire comes in the community, the ants make a ring around it, throwing formic acid on it from their bodies. The inside ants may perish but no one runs away.

Ants store their food for the winter in a peculiar way. Certain of them volunteer, or are conscripted, to become the Gem jars for the community and gorge themselves with "honeydew" and then hang themselves in the basement in even rows. There they remain until they are needed. Even if they die, they will perform this storage duty for the community. Another source of food is the growing of mushrooms in their basements. In our ants' house there are many cellar doors, which lead no doubt to the stables and storerooms. I would like to see them but I will not intrude. I hope they will observe the same rule with us.

We get along better when our association is not too close. Indeed I have made up my mind to get my information hereafter from books. Huber and Maeterlinck have done enough observing. When I linger around the nest, too many of them come away with me.

Maeterlinck says the ants are friendly to other ants if they have any odour of kinship at all, so I brought them a few from the peonies, just as a friendly gesture, and I was shocked at the treatment accorded to visiting delegates. There was one wild scramble to see who would get the first bite.

But one thing is certain. If anyone intends to destroy an ant house, it will have to be done before the assassin reads anything about them or even watches them. The ant is far less unhappy than the happiest of men. Their health is perfect; there are no epidemics among them; indigestion is unknown. They have no unemployment.

They are sensitive only to cold, but even cold does not kill them—it merely puts them to sleep. They ignore the law of gravity; they can walk on ceilings. They hardly know what it is to be dead, they come to life so easily. So how could anyone destroy this cone of contentment, this jumble of joy, in a world that has never had enough of either?

I carry out some sugar and scatter it about. Instantly, all operations cease. The community has proclaimed a holiday! Their lease has been renewed.

"BY CLOTHES I MEAN NOT
MERELY COVERING, BUT ADORNMENT."

> JULY 9, 1938

Much has been written about the buoyant spirits of the people of Saskatchewan and the gallant way they have borne their losses. But the half has never been told.

I attended a reception in March, in a part of Saskatchewan that has not had a crop for seven years. I thought it was a brave thing for them to do, for seven years must have worn them down well past the line of decency in dress. That is what I thought, in my ignorance.

I got my first surprise when I was in the hall. A tall vase of chrysanthemums greeted me. I touched them furtively. Yes, they were real. So were all the other flowers in the house. Home grown and beautiful! They even had a corsage bouquet for me, a pelargonium blossom, with pink oxalis, tied with silver ribbon.

I spoke of this, trying to let them know how highly they had honoured me, in cutting their precious flowers. They assured me the flowers had done well this year, and everyone had them.

I got my next surprise when I looked about me. The guests were dressed not only well but fashionably. They even had the queer little hats, resembling windmills, coffee-grinders, skimmers and tea-cozies, just exactly the sort of hats I had seen the week before in Toronto.

I wondered where they had come from. Had they all rich relatives who sent these things to them? Rich relatives usually send last year's garments, I believe. But these dresses were certainly all 1938 models (numbers is the word now). I knew they were enjoying my bewilderment, and now I know.

Saskatchewan has a university and in that university there is a professor of economics. And she and her assistants have travelled every gravelled highway or dirt road in Saskatchewan, giving the women of the province instruction in the finest art of all, the art of living. And that really means the art of making the best of one's environment. They have taught them to design and make their own clothes. By clothes I mean not merely covering, but adornment.

In the days before the drought, when money was plentiful, the farm women sent to the mail-order houses for their dresses. I have several old photographs of conventions I have attended, where the dresses were not distinctive. Two or three might be identical. I was in a series once myself. But you will not see any duplicates now. Out of the desert has come a gift, the gift of originality.

I wrote once, last year, of the conversations I heard in a Saskatchewan city when the wind, laden with dust, was raging through the streets. I said the people made no comment on the dust, but talked of poetry and music. This was in Regina.

A newspaper woman at the coast disagreed with me, rather violently. I think she said I was "havering," or words to that effect. She thought it could not be that people could rise above their environment and see a pleasant world beyond the dust.

There was nothing to do but take it, because, as Elbert Hubbard says, you cannot tell people anything unless they already know it.

83

But I hope she heard Sir Hugh Robertson's farewell address, just before he sailed for England, in which he gave his highest measure of praise to the children's chorus in Saskatchewan. Such artistry, he said, he had not heard in Canada, as when the Regina children sang of waterfalls they had never seen.

"Wake up, Vancouver," he said. "Wake up Victoria! You have but to lift your eyes to behold magic, but can it be that the eye of flesh can confuse the eye of the soul?"

Travelling across the country I saw here and there small bodies of water, looking like lakes where no lakes had been before. They were walled up on one or more sides, and were really lakes of artificial make, water-stops. Instead of letting the water run away in the spring, it was held here by those walls.

All over the prairie provinces may be seen projects for conserving the rainfall and increasing the water surface from which the clouds receive their moisture. Cattle are feeding on abundant meadows, some of the fields of grain are dimpling in the breeze, the plowed fields are richly brown, with an undertone of purple. I see that young trees have been planted to take the place of those that died in the drought. Saskatchewan is on its way back to prosperity.

In Saskatoon, I was taken to see an exhibition of pictures by a young Viennese, named Steiger. I wish they could be seen by everyone.

Steiger began his life in Canada by working for twenty-five dollars a month. He wrote show cards for a store and did some clerking. Now he is making pictures of people, and he has chosen the people around him.

He had just finished one of a man who sometimes comes to Saskatoon in his wanderings. He is a long-haired rover, with haunting blue eyes, filled with the old question of why do we suffer? With a pack on his back and his hands resting on a stick, his face, arresting and questioning, looked out at us. The hands, sunburnt to a mahogany shade, blue veined and somehow beautiful, fascinated me. Indeed the whole display is a soul-warming experience.

His picture called *Drought* has been produced in many Canadian papers. It shows a young man, sunburnt, weather-beaten, his eyes burning with disappointment and inflamed by the dust. Yet there is strength and power in his face. He has not yet admitted defeat. Steiger is an interpreter of the country as truly as if he had written a novel.

"WE ARE BACK AGAIN IN THE GOOD YEARS."

> JULY 23, 1938

The prairie blooms again! Its fertility is established; its good name is restored. The people who said the Great American Desert is creeping northward are now routed and silent. The prairie has come back!

Discretion makes me say that the crop is still in doubt. Naturally, there are dangers. Frost may wither it, rust corrode it, grasshoppers eat it, but one fact has been established. The prairie is still fertile.

Wild roses, wild strawberries, Saskatoon berries, tiger lilies, have all come out to bear their testimony. The prairie has repented of its evil ways and turned over a new leaf—a nice shiny green leaf, too. There is water in the lakes and sloughs, reflecting the white clouds in the blue sky, and over it the wild ducks draw fans and circles.

There is a festive feeling on the prairie now—a joviality that is part hope, part memory. We are back again in the Good Years. The Lean Years have folded up and departed. Here are dimpling fields of wheat, fat cattle on the lush meadows and colts in the pasture racing away from the train, pretending they are frightened.

The country is celebrating. It is the Feast of Demeter, the goddess of Earth, the Mother of Grain—who has turned to us after a long absence, with no questions asked.

I felt this when I visited in the two places in Manitoba where we had lived, Wawanesa and Manitou. The Black Creek still runs, full, brown and reedy, past the old Stopping House. The Souris River still flows over its bed of golden gravel on its way to the Assiniboine. The wild fruit has formed on the bushes; the roses on the headlands were never more fragrant.

But another generation has come. I saw new faces, strange faces—changed faces, everywhere. In Wawanesa I felt suddenly strange and lonely. I wanted to see the boys and girls of long ago ... Even the names on the stores were new. Life does not wait for any of us. However, I shall not speak of the past. The spirit remains and there are advancements. Pleasure has come to the countryside. Children passed us on bicycles singing, "Heigh-ho, heigh-ho, I'm off to Mexico!"

I saw tidy farmyards sown to grass, machine sheds where the machinery is sheltered from the weather, better cattle in the pastures. Not so many in number but of better stock. Again there are horses on the land, fine six-horse teams turning down the weeds.

The trees have grown. Many of the farmhouses are hidden by the shelter belts, grown from the seedlings given away by the Dominion Experimental Farms years ago.

A few bare houses still stand treeless and grim, a mute commentary on the character of their owners—the people who could not be bothered with trees. These houses look sad and frustrated, and speak of defeat and possible family rows. The majority of women have wanted trees and flowers, just as they crave bright curtains and pretty china. But there comes a time when they cease to struggle, without, unfortunately, ceasing to care.

It was queer to travel the highway and see the houses, whose people I knew so many years ago.

There has always been a healthy, rugged independence about the country people, overlooked by some of the writers who have drawn their pictures of rural life in drab colours, missing the real meaning in the lives of the people. This spirit has always characterized Manitou— the little town I know best of all, for we lived here for twenty years.

Manitou has been an educational centre since its beginning, and even when the Normal School was closed recently, it went on independently. The citizens organized a "Youth Training Course," without outside help. Young people from the farms were invited to come in and register. The Normal School building, with its numerous classrooms, was used and the classes went on each day for three months.

The United Church minister's wife, who was a nurse, gave health lectures; the Anglican minister's wife lectured in domestic science and gave cooking lessons. Manitou has three master farmers and they conducted courses in agrarian subjects.

Samuel Magee, the veteran architect and builder, turned over his well-equipped shop to the boys who wanted to learn his art and showed them the way to construct farm buildings. An Austrian blacksmith taught the farm boys the tricks of welding and soldering and a harness-maker contributed his part in teaching the lads to mend and make hames and tugs and collars.

The furniture dealer, who is a man of wide learning, conducted "current events" classes. One of the choir leaders organized singing classes; the banker's wife conducted book reviews. The girls were taught the art of sewing, basket-making, rug-making and entertaining.

Everyone gave their services freely. It was a community effort to help the boys and girls on the farm to do their work with greater skill and pleasure.

"It was lots of fun," one of the leaders told me, "and we expect to do it again. A finer lot of young people I never met, keen and appreciative."

I remember when I went there at the age of sixteen, I was a frequenter of the WCTU Reading Room and Library, which was the scene of many discussions and debates. The frivolous-minded ones were set to playing games in one room, crokinole, checkers, authors; but the intelligentsia plodded through the *Review of Reviews*, *Scribner's*, *Montreal Witness* and the *Family Herald*, or read Marie Corelli's *A Romance of Two Worlds*, and argued about the immortality of the soul, the relative merits of science and literature as character builders, and whether or not conscience is an infallible guide.

When I travelled back to Winnipeg on the train from Manitou, I met a woman who told me her father, who lived near Roland, had mortgaged his farm to finance a church in his neighbourhood, forty years ago. (No, he did not lose his farm; the church people paid him back).

Knowing how a thrifty farmer dreads a mortgage, I can understand this man's courage. But he believed a church was needed in his community—he believed it passionately and so risked his home to bring it about.

And that, after all, is what we need today to solve all our problems. People who believe, not in any bland, anemic way, but with courage and self-sacrifice. People who will take a gambler's chance that the promises of God still stand!

"SEA AND SKY AND GREEN MEADOW,
WITH CATTLE ON THE LAND, AND SHIPS ON THE SEA."

> AUGUST 27, 1938

The visitor to Nova Scotia is always advised to see the South Shore, and looking at the picture of it, which I did as I travelled down from Sackville, I wondered if anything could be as beautiful as Mahone Bay with its 365 islands.

I read what President Roosevelt said about it—he had spoken of the "unhurried ways of the fisherfolk." Ramsay MacDonald had called it the "land of heart's desire," and wondered why he had missed it for so long. Dr. Brinkley of Del Rio, Texas, had caught a tuna weighing 758 pounds, off the coast at Liverpool [in Nova Scotia].

A woman to whom I had been speaking on the train, a Lunenburg woman, looked at me enviously when I said I was on my way to Nova Scotia for my first visit.

"I wish I could see Lunenburg harbour for the first time," she said, "when the ships return and the masts stand up like a forest!"

She told me something about the coastline, with its indentations and its coves and creeks.

"The paved road has done a lot for the people," she said. "I am not one that wants to keep the fisherfolk as primitive as they were in some places just to make the tourists stare and rave about them.

I want them to have some comforts, too, and now they are getting them, even radios and tablecloths.

"There are places along the South Shore where the people lived on fish and potatoes," she went on, "never bothering with other vegetables, but with tourists coming and wanting meals, they began to make gardens and live better, in every way."

Her maid lives in one of these places and she had heard about it from her.

"The women work in the hayfields with the men. Mary says she won't take her holidays until the haying is over. Her two sisters work in Boston and have learned American ways but when they come home, they do what father says. When father says, 'We'll make hay,' they make hay! And they daren't talk back to him."

The heavy father who can rule his household may have gone from other parts of Canada, but he still rules in some of the fishing villages on the South Shore.

We motored from Windsor to Chester, through upper Falmouth, following the Avon River until we saw where it had its source. The streams here, no longer subject to the tide, are clear and dark as if the colour of the trout has dyed the water. The road we travelled is winding and narrow in places but in good condition, as well made. Drinking troughs along the way remind us that much of the transportation has been done by ox-teams, though we saw only two or three of these bringing out loads of hay. The heavy rains have damaged the hay crop but there is already a fine crop of after-grass.

We passed some beautiful orchards before we reached the heavily wooded country and I was interested to see the space between the rows of trees was planted with buckwheat, now in full bloom. This will be cut and left on the ground for a mulch. I wondered why the ground was not cultivated, but the sod-culture is in favour now and appears to be successful, for the trees are well set with fruit.

At Chester, the bay was all I had hoped and more. Peace lay on the water and on the islands that led the eye step by step out to the open sea.

After leaving Mahone Bay we saw many berry pickers offering baskets of blueberries for sale. There were stands beside the road where lovely water lilies in crocks could be bought. Signs told us that handmade rugs and quilts were ready for us, and about this time we began to notice that we were crossing the railway track very often.

That is true of the whole South Shore. The highway and railway track seem to vie with each other in showing the traveller everything that is to be seen. No one can see it all, but we drove slowly and did our best.

Little sheltered coves, with canoes at anchor; beaches of pure red sand, where people lay in the sun; a party of picnickers opening their baskets; a woman on the veranda of a lovely white house reading a newspaper; two women driving by with a horse and covered buggy (I am sure they had a lap-robe embroidered in chain stitch); a white house with rain barrels at each side, painted white, too; fish drying on the shore in front of Frolic School; cobblestone houses at Dublin Shore and then the sign, "railway crossing three hundred feet, speed limit fifteen miles an hour"; and always the sea with its fishing boats, steamers and at least one lovely yacht with gleaming sails.

Near Petite Riviere we got to the honeysuckle county—great hedges of it, fragrant and beautiful. We left the railway track for a while, travelling on a good gravelled road. We smelled the odour of linden trees and saw roses on lawns, supported by leaning trellises.

At Liverpool, we stopped for supper at a neat little restaurant where tourists with bandana handkerchiefs on their heads sat at the next table. We wanted to reach Lockeport for the night, but a fog settled in from the sea and we stayed at White Point Beach, where the great rollers of the Atlantic threw spray on the rocks and filled the air with a sound so much like a heavy rain that every time I wakened, I had to resist the impulse to get up and shut the windows all over the house.

The next day, in spite of some fog and rain, we caught glimpses of great beauty. Sea and sky and green meadow, with cattle on the land, and ships on the sea. We had a good map with us and had been looking ahead for a place to have lunch.

We agreed the Pubnicos should be seen—there are so many of them, all in a row, on both shores of Pubnico harbour. There is Lower East, Middle West and West Pubnico, and the same number of East Pubnicos, and at the head of the harbour Pubnico itself. These are on the map.

In reality there are Mids and Centrals as well. But we had a good lobster salad with the Amiraults there, I think it was at Mid East Pubnico, in a neat little restaurant which displayed a sign that "no intoxicating liquor would be tolerated on the premises." The proprietor told us liquor "makes plenty trouble," and we agreed with her. The Highway Department is with her, too.

The window of the little handicraft shop in Pubnico is made into a winter scene, with salt for snow and little houses made of bark and ox teams carved from wood, drawing loads of logs. Inside the shop there are pictures made by a needle instead of a brush, with wool instead of paint and with carved frames.

We saw two of the Amirault family here, who told us these handicrafts are carried on by the women in the winter, the design handed down from mother to daughter. They invited us to visit the museum nearby but rain was threatening and we pushed on, crossed the railway at Pubnico, just plain Pubnico, and then went on to Yarmouth.

"THERE IS SOMETHING ABOUT THE SEA THAT LOOSENS PEOPLE'S TONGUES AND DRAWS THEM INTO A CLOSE FELLOWSHIP."

> SEPTEMBER 24, 1938

There is something about the sea that loosens people's tongues and draws them into a close fellowship. Perhaps it is its immensity that shrinks us down to atoms, its cold indifference that drives us to seek human companionship.

There is no doubt that at sea people grow sociable, friendly and communicative. It begins when the vessel leaves the dock and the yellow, blue and red streamers that billow in the wind grow tighter, stretch and break, and the faces on shore grow smaller and smaller and at last run together in a blur, like the memories of the past.

I never like these drawn-out partings. I think we should say goodbye and walk away without looking back. But far be it from me to deny anyone the right to dramatize their emotions if it eases the strain in a time like this.

An ocean crossing is nothing now. Five days of luxurious life on a beautiful ship with a morning paper appearing mysteriously inside your cabin door, a radio in the lounge, concerts at night, a moving picture afternoon and evening, a library for the studious and a nursery for the children.

Strange meetings take place on shipboard, and we had one of them. One of the men at our table had the prospectus of a mine in the north, which a friend of his had handed him, asking him to look it over when he was on the boat. The story of the finding of the mine was interesting and he told us about it.

A sailor's boat had been frozen-in on an island and he had supposedly gone out with a pick to see what he could find. Evidently, he knew something of ores, for he gave samples to someone who was coming out.

The ores proved to be valuable . . . But the man who brought them out did not know the sailor's name—and there seemed to be no way of finding him.

A young man at the table suddenly became interested in the story and asked a few questions, which revealed an intimate knowledge of the island and the circumstances. He was the sailor! From him we heard the best stories of the whole journey, for his are stories that have no end.

It explains, too, a reason for his having forgotten about the ore he found. He has had other interests since then. He has been prospecting in another field.

It began in the north and under thrilling circumstances. He and two other men were adrift on a northern lake, their boat had begun to leak and there was nothing they could do. It looked like the end and an unpleasant one at that.

They had letters and parcels for people along the way, letters and parcels that would not be delivered. As they waited for the end, he opened one of the parcels, which contained a book. After all, to read a book was as good a way as any to spend the last hours.

The book contained a new thought that God has a plan for every life, and as he read, it seemed to him that he must not die—there was too great a reason for living. There must be some way of escape.

And there was! Strange, unbelievable escape from dangers, on the water on a 750-mile trek in winter weather—back to civilization.

Now it might be by chance that they were saved, that the ice went out half an hour after they passed over it, it might be by chance that they recovered from "teepee fever" just by lying in their sleeping bags, it might be by chance that they escaped the storms and found their way in a trackless wilderness.

But the next story he told us could not have happened by chance. It was a story of West Ham, in London, and it has to do with the changing of a man's heart. Changing the wind and the weather must be child's play when compared with changing a bitter heart into a loving one. The wind does not care much which way it blows. One direction is as good as another.

This is the story:

Bill Rowell of West Ham, London, was a communist leader who hated parsons and policemen. He saw them and all those in authority as brutes and tyrants, and the police were afraid of him.

One night a young man, a peer's son, knocked on Bill's door and got in. Bill did not know he was a peer's son. It did not show in his face or in his dress.

The two young men discussed the problems of life. Bill liked the other young man's frankness and the way he admitted his own faults. As a result of that meeting, the peer's son went to live with Bill. There was no spare bed, so he put two chairs together and slept on them. He showed Bill a new way of serving his country and Bill, being honest, decided to give it a try.

Now Bill Rowell is a leader in a new sense. He is leading people to understand each other, to help each other. His communist friends thought at first that Bill had turned soft and deserted them, and they were ready to kill him. Now the whole district has been changed.

The unemployed say that Bill is doing more for them now than he ever did before. Instead of attacking society, now he is changing it.

The news of Bill Rowell spread to the British House of Commons, where one Conservative MP told the story and said that Bill had shown him that if he wanted a new England he would have to start to change his own party. Fourteen members of the party immediately sent out a letter asking the others to come to a weekend gathering to discuss a plan whereby God would be given control in their lives.

Good is just as contagious as evil, and this is why I said this story is the kind that has no end! We have all sung about redeeming love and committed verses to memory about the "faith that moves mountains." Miracles should not surprise us. But they do.

This type of friendship takes time and energy, tact and understanding. And we still have our problems of unemployment. One person in every twenty is dependent on the other nineteen. And yet the Minister of Transport has recently said that there may soon be a labour shortage in Canada. He means, of course, a shortage of trained labour ...

Our people are our glory and our wealth. The very essence of democracy and Christianity lies in the value of the individual. Germany and Russia stand convicted before the whole world in their disregard for human life. They sacrifice human beings without mercy, turning back the clock of civilization to the Dark Ages.

"WHAT IS WRONG WITH YOUNG CANADA THAT IT WILL NOT DO ANYTHING HEROIC FOR ITS COUNTRY'S GOOD?"

> NOVEMBER 26, 1938

When I was in Winnipeg, I was told about a serious condition which exists in the city schools. Meetings are being held in the school auditoriums of Nazis and of Communists, where the German system and the Russian system are being exalted. No one seems to know just what to do about it.

Suppression seems to be the only thing, but suppression indicates fear. Are we really afraid of the Nazi system of government or of the platform of the Communist? If either of these is better than the Christian democratic system, why should we not admit it? But they are not better.

These systems, successful as they are in some respects, should hold no terrors for us, for we know something better—but because of natural laziness we are a bit upset about having to defend our ideals. We hate to be bothered. So naturally our reaction is to stop these meetings by force. It's so much easier than argument or demonstration and could be done by the police without any effort on our part. What are police for, anyway?

We might just as well face the situation. Christian democracy has to be fought for, but not with guns or bombs, deportation or imprisonment. These are outdated weapons. We must revive the history of liberty and make it a living faith. We must show our boys and girls that there is romance, adventure and glamour in the good life, in freedom of speech, in being a good neighbour, in the Golden Rule and in moral rearmament. We must admit our failures and show the way to national unity.

Herr Hitler has laid his hand on the shoulder of German youth and electrified them into action for the purpose of creating a dominant Germany, able to force its will on smaller nations. He has set them hiking, singing, marching, to develop their physical fitness; he was able to make the people renounce the pleasures of good food so they could pay for weapons, and the young people voluntarily deny themselves tobacco or beer as a means of developing strong muscles.

What is wrong with young Canada that it will not do anything heroic for its country's good?

Let us be fair to our youth; they are exactly like their elders. We have all had so much done for us that we simply accept it as our right. Gratitude looks like sentimentalism. We do not value freedom of speech because we have always had it. We have not enough imagination to see that by our indifference and selfishness we may lose what we have. The aggressive groups will win, unless we move and move quickly.

What we should promote in our schools to offset the Nazis and Communists is a series of programs so vital, compelling and attractive that the pendulum will swing our way. Christianity has in it every good thing in either of these and none of their weaknesses or cruelties. Beside this, it has the dynamic which gives power. The power of God is the greatest force in the world and we have not yet explored it.

Spiritually, we are still underdeveloped. We are at the place in our spiritual history that the natural world was in just before electricity was discovered. We are still experimenting with the pieces of flannel, rubbed on amber. We are lighting fires by rubbing dry sticks together. We are trying to read by the light of tallow candles.

We need a real awakening. We must look around us and see how foolishly we behave.

Here we are drugging ourselves with liquor, killing ourselves at the rate of thousands per year in accidents attributable to liquor, losing mental and moral strength because we haven't the courage and backbone to break away from a foolish, expensive and dangerous social custom.

Look at our divisions, our petty jealousies. We are such individualists filled with pride that we mistake the setting for the jewel, and unless enlightenment comes through our own channel we will have none of it.

We must lay aside all these fetters, for fetters they are, and mobilize our people for the great adventure. We have a greater country, a greater tradition, a greater opportunity than any of the dictator countries, for we have room. We have friendship. We have the good will of our neighbours. We have God. Not the tribal God, as many have misunderstood Him, but the God of all mankind, who plays no favourites and who once came to Earth to show us how to live.

I believe that a direct program of Christian democratic education in our homes, in our schools, in our churches and societies and colleges, wherein our writers, musicians, teachers, ministers, parents and children are all enlisted, will solve all our problems, and do it quickly. We have all the machinery ready. We need only the awakened spirit.

We have to sell democracy to our own people. We must convince them that democracy has to be intelligent. Democracy has to have a spiritual force behind it or it falls before the first temptation.

If we are content to live selfishly and stupidly, a dictatorship is the best form of government for us. A dictator does not want the individual to think. Those who think are dealt with. A dictatorship calls for obedience only—do as you are told and ask no questions!

Knowing Canadians as I do, I believe we want to possess our own souls. Are we ready for the question?

"LET THE HURRICANE ROAR!
THE KALE HAS NO FEARS, WITH ITS TOUGH FIBRE."

> DECEMBER 3, 1938

Summer waited at Lantern Lane until I came back from Europe. All the way across the prairie I saw it fading, and the flowers disappearing.

The prairie scene was one of cold beauty; plowed fields purple in the sunlight, ridged into a pattern by the cultivator; the stubble fields bleached into pale gold, broken by piles of new straw where cattle and horses foraged and pigs burrowed.

The prairie has had a long breathing spell under clear skies this year, with unbroken weather for weeks. Lovely days of sun and quiet nights of stars, but even this does not satisfy everyone and complaints are heard about the continued dryness. The ground is too hard for plowing and if the ground freezes dry, winter's snow will do us no good, for the moisture will not penetrate the hard surface.

The warm days have set the willows thinking of spring and the rising sap has coloured them purple and red in a glow of false hope, but some of these nights the poor little things will feel a hand of lead laid on their hearts and they will remember what season it is!

When we left Elkhorn [Manitoba], we saw the first trace of snow, just fine powdering on the plowed fields and enough to outline the roads that ran through the stubble. The hummocks in the fair-rings were covered, too, suggesting the old-fashioned bun-cushions that lay on many a horsehair sofa in the early 1890s.

Sunrise on the mountains, as we approached Calgary, is an experience that atones for many of life's dull places. Sun-lighted snow peaks, moving blue shadows of stormy clouds drifting across them, now lifting, now settling; windows of farmhouses, catching the sunshine and darting out rays of light that seem like signals; the rolling landscape that seems to flow into the mountains like an inland sea, carpeted with tawny grass—it all makes a scene that hushes conversation.

I saw it on a frosty morning, when the smoke from the farm-houses rose straight into the still air. Not a wind was stirring as we came into the city, but behind the nearest peaks we could see a snowstorm coming, which soon shut off our view.

In Vancouver there was a white frost on the sidewalks and many of the garden flowers were limp and dead. I felt a little sorry for myself that all the beauty would be gone from Lantern Lane. I might have known that summer lingers longer on the Island than anywhere else.

So here I am, the first morning, going around to see the survi-vors and they are many. Red leaves still glow on the sumacs and three fine blossoms sway from the high stalks of the California tree-poppy. They are not quite as big as they were in the summer, but would do well on a hat yet, with their silky white leaves and yellow centre. "Poached eggs" is the popular name and describes them well.

The newest flower in the garden is the yellow jasmine, which should not bloom until January, but here it is, fluffy and full, with its little bell-like flowers, in defiance of every seed catalogue and calendar, exulting in its self-determination. It is growing into a lovely shrub and now covers the middle part of the front veranda.

One hollyhock holds up its head and waves a lovely wine-red corsage in the gentle breeze which passes by. The same breeze rings the blue Canterbury bells in their second or third blooming and brushes the firmly set dahlias in yellow and purple closely packed pom-poms. There are single blossoms, too, in rose and magenta, marred a little by wind and weather, but brilliant as ever in their colour and texture.

I often thought of the red sunflowers which were in full bloom when I left, lovely big ones with strong markings, and some distinctly red. The birds came by the hundreds when the seed was ripe, but we have enough to sow again, for these are precious, not only for their beauty but because of the giver.

Jim Clarke of Winnipeg came to the station one day last year to give me a little bag of seeds . . . and now Jim has gone. But the seeds he sowed in the lives of his family and friends will go on blooming, like the sunflowers, for Jim had the gift of healing laughter and the mirth that has no bitterness.

In the vegetable garden, the kale is a lovely sight, with its closely curled leaves, dark green and vigorous. Let the hurricane roar! The kale has no fears, with its tough fibre.

The peppers are still on the stalks, a lovely crop, burning red now in patches. I picked a big glossy one with a dash of red coming on its cheek and have it on my desk trying to regain the pleasure I had to miss by being away so long. The eggplants struggled through, but no one seems to think much of them, even when they ripened.

The grape vine is wrinkled and withered, but the grapes are in jars in the basement, made into jelly that "will stand alone." So are the blackberries and some of the neighbour's logans.

The shelves in the basement throw out a satisfying vibration of security and remind me of the collars of corn I saw under the eaves of the houses in Savoy and Burgundy. The same vibration is in the little root house, where the onions and potatoes are stored.

There are also citrons in their green leopard skins and a few fine, long vegetable marrows, each of which will make a "Gordon Head Goose" when filled with meat, rice and onions. There are boxes of apples in the apple house and boxes of lavender, and the carrots big as turnips are still growing in Mr. Edwards's field. We ate some of them yesterday, for we still enjoy extra-territorial rights in this field.

The house is full of gladioli—the last of a long procession of bloom—and two fine roses, a talisman and a crimson beauty whose name I do not know, bloom in a vase on my desk. So am I right in believing that the summer of 1938 stayed to wave a kindly hand to me before it passed forever away into the land of memory.

The cover crops are green and beautiful now. Mr. Towler's alfalfa runs up and down the field in even rows—chrysanthemums in great blocks of colour dot the landscape. Lantern Lane is carpeted with autumn leaves and more are falling as the wind comes in from the sea.

The wood piles have grown since I left. So has the little Coronation oak tree from Great Windsor Park. It has three sets of leaves on it now and no longer needs a stake to show its location.

Across the road the great pines still stand, gently bending without haste, or confusion, or resentment. They know something, these evergreens, that makes them able to bend, without loss of dignity, beauty or pride.

"THERE IT STANDS, BEAUTIFUL AND TRAGIC."

> MARCH 4, 1939

When I attended the League of Nations Assembly last September, I felt that it was a high privilege to see mankind's great experiment for peace—even if it had temporarily failed.

The beautiful building, gleaming white on the grassy lawns that run down to the blue waters of Lake Geneva, looks like a palace of peace. Inside may be seen South African veined wood, Australian walnut, Finnish granite, Italian and Swedish marble, African pear-wood; the government of Iran gave Persian carpets; India sent green-wood furniture for the president's room; Latvia gave woodwork of satin smoothness; Luxembourg gave the bronze gates of the main entrance to the assembly building; Czechoslovakia arranged, decorated and furnished the room for the permanent delegates at Geneva.

The Hungarian government gave tapestries, so did Belgium and Spain, and France sent pictures. The United Kingdom gave the bas-reliefs of the council ante-room. Switzerland donated wall paintings and frescoes. The building cost 29.5 million Swiss francs, which is about seven million dollars, not including the cost of the library, which was presented by John D. Rockefeller at a cost of two million dollars.

There it stands, beautiful and tragic. The six hundred members of the secretariat are chosen from many countries. They are able and expert and are doing good work for the world, quietly but efficiently.

The papers recently announced that the Nutrition Committee in Canada, set up last year by the League of Nations, has sent in its report. This is new in our history—to have a definite inspection of our eating habits. (I do not mean table manners.) The Nutrition Committee have had inspectors in representative cities and country places, making inquiries and tabulating returns.

They have found that we do not use enough milk, butter and eggs. They find that sixty per cent of the people on relief in cities do not use milk at all. Their report is available for us, and no doubt it will affect the farm products of Canada.

I hope the Nutrition Committee will recommend lowered tariffs on fruit during the season when green vegetables are hard to get and lower freight rates between east and west, so that BC fruit may be exchanged easily for prairie grain, to the advantage of both. The Nutrition Committee is an attempt to bring expert advice to the problem of food across our country.

When I said the League is tragic, I refer to its inability to keep peace. In spite of its covenant, its signatories (of which Canada is one), its experts, its advisers, its surveys, its library of 240,000 volumes. The League is like a beautiful house with every known mechanical device, crystal chandeliers, lights in every hallway, in every closet, over every door and on the lawns—every electrical device, vacuum cleaners, fireplaces, air-conditioning—everything, but electricity to set them in motion. One thing lacking, only one.

In the case of the League it is power. The power of honesty, courage, fair dealing and the driving impulse to observe the Golden Rule. It is too easy to say the failure of the United States to take responsibility killed the League, or that the greed of Germany and Italy and Japan killed the League.

It goes deeper than that. No one nation did it. We all did it.

I had this in my mind when I came back to Canada. I had seen people in the grip of fear, kindly people who love their homes, their children, decency, music, poetry, all the amenities of life. I saw them twisted and torn with fear.

When I came back to Canada on October 7, it was a bright autumn day, and the sun shone bright on the blue St. Lawrence River. The maple leaves had turned to crimson—cattle grazed on the green after-grass—smoke rose from peaceful homes of contentment and security. It was good to be back. But I could not forget what I had seen. I had looked into the cauldron of war—I had seen fear, cold fear, laying its heavy hand on innocent and helpless people.

Now, what have we to do with this? Canada is remote from Europe. We have the protection of two strong nations. We have a proud record from the last war. We gave up sixty thousand of our best men to fight the war to end wars. Can't we let it go at that, and dig in and be comfortable?

One of the delegates from a South American republic said something like this to me. He said: "Europe is doomed. They have no principles now. They have only hatreds. Why should we go down with them?"

There's the isolationist attitude, and it has no appeal to me. I think of Conrad's *Lord Jim*, where the hero saved his own life when the ship sank, but had no pleasure in it, haunted by a ghost of memory and remorse. When a situation of danger arose again, though he could have saved himself without blame, he did not take the safe way.

"This time," he said, "I will go down with the ship."

Canada is made up of people whose ancestors came from Europe. Adventurous souls, seeking liberty of conscience, freedom of action, homes of their own. They were ready to accept hardship, cold and hunger for the right to be free. They paid a heavy price for liberty, but liberty is worth what it costs.

That day, when my heart was warm with the joy of return, I had a new vision of my country. Canada is a land of destiny. It can give a lead to the liberty-loving people of the world, if the flame of adventure is still burning brightly enough to shed a light in dark places, and if we are willing to pay the price.

Canada cannot choose any easy way, nor any selfish policy of isolation. She must be willing to go down with the ship. If the ship goes down. The countries of the world are bound together for good or evil. The festering wounds of Spain and China throb in our hearts.

Dr. Wellington Koo, at the League of Nations, told us this. He said you may not think it matters that there is war in China, war in Spain, war in Palestine. But it does, for war is like blood poisoning.

Now, then, what can we do about it? What can we do here to help in the healing of the nations?

We naturally think of our territory. We have room. Room is wealth. We cannot feel virtuous about holding our country for ourselves just from motives of selfishness. So we dress up our case with reasons.

We say we cannot "take in Jewish refugees, because they always flock into cities, and the only place we have room for people is on the farms." As a matter of fact, there are many evidences that Jewish people do go on farms and make a success of agriculture.

Jews from Austria and Germany, with their knowledge of chemicals, glove-making, colour-printing, scientific instruments, etc., could introduce and develop in Canada the manufacture of articles that we now import. The Jewish refugees in London have made that city the centre of the fur business, instead of Leipzig.

We have ceramic clay in Canada for pottery and glass, and there are skilled people anxious to come to us, with all their secrets. Think what that would mean.

Refugees have enriched many countries. They would enrich us.

Whether they enrich us or not materially, one thing is certain: If we refuse them, we will be impoverished in our hearts.

iii. Writers and Writing

Although **Nellie McClung** *is remembered as a social activist first and a writer second, her love of literature predates her commitment to social justice. When she was a young girl in rural Manitoba, Nellie's world was opened up by books and she dreamed of becoming an author. By the time she and Wes settled on Vancouver Island, Nellie was a bestselling author many times over, and she was still profoundly influenced by the books that she read.*

Books and authors made an appearance in several of Nellie's columns, a few of which are included in the following pages. If we are to

take anything from these columns, it is that Nellie thought a lot about what she read. Books had personal meaning to her, but they also had political meaning. As the world descended into war and books became symbols of cultural expression, the state control over reading material in Nazi Germany upset Nellie greatly. To her, the burning of books was a crime against humanity. "Books are the best ambassadors," she writes in her Christmas column of 1940. "They bind us to our fellow man more securely than treaties."

In the column that ran on December 7, 1940, Nellie writes about a book produced by the students at Inkameep Day School, members of the Osoyoos First Nation near Oliver, BC, from 1932 to 1942. These children were fortunate to have a teacher named Anthony Walsh, who fostered his pupils' creativity while showing deep respect for their families and culture.

"THINGS HAVE A DREADFUL
PERMANENCE WHEN PEOPLE DIE."

> JULY 24, 1937

There is a substantial stone house on Ash Road [near Lantern Lane] in Gordon Head that looks out across an orchard to the sea. In one season it becomes a show place where garden lovers come to gladden their eyes with the sight of a whole field of languorous regal lilies, whose petals are thick and soft as duchesse satin.

The house is made of dressed stone, quarried and cut by the owner, who took the stones of his own land and lovingly fashioned them for the building of his home, spending five years in doing it. The house, which is a large and handsome one, is finished inside with Douglas fir, also home grown, and every vibration in it gives a feeling of home and harmony.

Things have a dreadful permanence when people die. So it is with the stone house, which now stands solid, secure and ageless [while] the skilful hand that fashioned it has turned to dust.

However, George Watson's memory will be green and fragrant for many years to come, for he has left other monuments that, like the stone house, will resist the erosion of time. He served this community long and well in many capacities. While he was a member of the council of Saanich, he was closely identified with the march of progress and it was he who fought for the water supply that we enjoy here now. "Watson and Water" was the slogan at many an election.

Banshee Lane, a delightful woodland path, was given to the people of this neighbourhood by George Watson, who bought a strip of land fifteen feet wide and almost a quarter of a mile long, and another neighbour, Miss Finlayson, who donated fifteen feet beside it, from Ferndale Road down to the sea. So this became a path to the beach for all the children of the neighbourhood, and Watson stipulated when the gift was made that this would always be a path and not a motor road, so the young bathers who run down to Margaret's Bay now with their towels under their arms run safely.

On June 19, my mind suddenly turned to the stone house on Ash Road, when over the radio I heard that Sir James Barrie [author of *Peter Pan*] had just died in London. I knew the message would bring "muckle" grief to the family there, for the name on the gate is "Thrums."

I went over to see Mrs. Watson and Marjorie, her daughter, that night, when the word came. The rain was streaking the windows and guttering down the drains to make ponds in the freshly plowed land. Ferndale Road was shining like a mirror, and though the night was heavy with clouds, the long summer evening was still light.

It seemed fitting that the sky should be sorrowing for the passing of James M. Barrie, that spirit of the Eternal Child who had "plucked at the skirts of the grey old world all these years, coaxing her to come and play with him," the strange little Pied Piper whose sweet music has set all our hearts dancing.

"My husband was James Barrie's cousin," Mrs. Watson said, "and he, too, was born at Kirriemuir [Scotland] and in the same tenement. The Barries lived at one end and the Watsons at the other. My husband was ten years younger than James, but age was nothing to James.

"All the children and young people loved him, and when he came back from London it was like a visit of royalty, and him so humble and sweet and always a little sad, as if the world, even with all its applause and success, was a perplexing place after all. But he always had stories for the children and he was full of games and fancies!"

Two of Watson's sisters had gone from Canada and had visited at Barrie's London house on Robert Street, where he lived with his wife for fifteen years, and had received a warm welcome both from Sir James and Mary Ansell, his wife. She was a lovely woman, much younger than James, and the Watson sisters had nothing but good words for her, though they could see neither of them were happy. In some ways, James was always a child and in other ways an old man but always the soul of kindness, and when his wife left him he gave her two houses and a great fortune.

Then we talked about his books and what wonderful women he had created in them.

"And they are all patterned after his mother, Margaret Ogilvy," Mrs. Watson said. "And my husband said his picture of her was exactly to the life."

We talked about his love of children and of how he had adopted a family of three boys, one of whom was killed in the war and one lost his life in a drowning accident, but the third one, Peter Davies, was the man who sat with him in the end; and of how he dealt so kindly with women in his books, even the Painted Lady of Double Dykes with her graceful little airs. When profanity poured from her lips, he said, she "swore like a bairn who had been in ill company."

"Scottish women are independent and resourceful," Mrs. Watson said. "Reverence, independence and backbone were the cardinal virtues of these humble folk."

Our talk shifted then to the beginnings of the Gordon Head settlement and of how she and George thought nothing of putting the baby in the buggy and coming out from town, six miles through the bush. Her people, the Grants, who still live here, owned many acres of this lovely country. This was long before the forest was cleared away.

On one of these six-mile trips, the Watsons saw the spot on which the stone house stands and suddenly knew it for their home, but it wasn't for sale. Some man had built a little house there and called it "Jersey Hall," but he was gone and no one knew who had the selling of the land.

But one day, Willie, her brother, came in to see them in town and announced that "Jersey Hall was for sale, and if they did not buy it, he would." He named the price, at which George Watson exclaimed: "It might as well be a million. We haven't the money."

She said: "We'll take the place, Willie, but first I have to put my bread in the pans. I'll go and see about it then."

"By night," she went on, with a quiet chuckle, "it was ours."

"And where did you get the money?" I asked, forgetting my manners in my interest.

"I had it by me," she said. "I saved ten dollars here, five dollars there, and we all had a little income from Scotland when we came. I just put mine by, thinking I might need it for something. No, George did not know about it and he never asked."

Barrie did not create the resourceful, keen-witted Scottish women who grace his pages—he merely recorded them!

"SHE IS A RADICAL, REALLY."

have a great treasure in my possession now, a book just one hundred years old, entitled *The Women of England* and written by a woman. Her name appears as "Mrs. Ellis" on the title page but in the comparative privacy of the preface she signs herself "Sarah Stickney Ellis."

The writer of this interesting old book was no doubt considered an advanced woman in her day. She is a radical, really. She advocated the dignity of labour in any sphere of life and urged her readers to study the art of conversation. She poured indignation on the women who take pride in their ignorance of everyday life. She believed that women cannot know too much but warns them not to parade their knowledge if they would appeal to men . . .

In her chapter on conversation she makes a curious reference to Nootka Sound, saying there are women who never know north from south and if one were to ask them which way the wind is blowing, the expectation of a correct answer would be much the same as "if they were asked to tell whether the tide was at that moment rising or falling in Nootka Sound." It is curious that she should have had Nootka Sound in her mind . . .

This book is a model of good book-binding and careful handling. There is not a wrinkled leaf. Bound in black leather with gold edges. I wonder if any of our books will be read a hundred years from now!

The owner of the book was Alexandrina H. Bury, who evidently received it for a New Year's gift in 1842.

"IT IS STRANGE ABOUT POETRY AND HOW BLIND WE ARE TO ITS VALUE AND HOW SUBLIMELY CARELESS WE ARE OF OUR POETS."

> DECEMBER 7, 1940

I n Germany, black silence is surely falling on the people, for no church bells ring, no dogs bark, no birds sing and even the radios go off early in the evening because of the air raids. Fannie Hurst in her autobiography, *Peculiar Treasure*, made the statement that not one line of music or poetry has been written in Germany since 1935. What could they write about, these stifled people, who must not presume to express an opinion? They cannot mourn their fallen, nor even inquire for their men. Germany has accomplished a complete mental black-out of her people.

Men of evil desire, who come into power, always try to silence the poet and writer, fearing them more than any other. Thomas Mann, who had to leave Germany, has written one of the undying letters of all times in his farewell to the University of Bonn.

God help our darkened and desecrated country, he writes. To what a pass, in less than four years, have they brought Germany! Ruined, sucked dry in body and soul by armaments with which to threaten the world; loved by nobody, regarded with fear and cold aversion by all, it stands on the brink of disaster, while its enemies stretch out hands to snatch back so important a member of the future family of nations if it would only come to its senses and try to understand the real needs of this moment.

Germany has lost her voice, her mind and her soul, and if she can work her fatal purpose the same paralysis will fall on all of us. But we thank God that the free spirit of man still lives and finds expression. The free people of the world were never more articulate. We have profited by Germany's losses. Many European writers are now on this continent or in England.

Louis Golding, who can no longer write in the countries where his past life has been spent, now writes for us *The World I Knew*. He tells how in days gone by, he roamed the world; then saw that his world was shrinking; at last he had but London and Paris then London. Mr. Golding, who is a Jew and the author of that unforgettable book *Mr. Emmanuel*, writes without bitterness but with a great longing that the agony of Central Europe should be assuaged. His book closes with these words: "You have made a beautiful world, O God, but not a wise one."

Sigrid Undset, Nobel Prize winner from Norway, whose voice was heard on the radio a few weeks ago, is an exile on this continent and she has a book this year. André Maurois and Hendrik van Loon are on this side of the water, too. There are dozens of others, whose coming will enrich our lives and literature.

But I want to write especially of the blossoming of our own people in these evil days. Rose Macaulay in a recent issue of the *Saturday Evening Post* describes the air-raid shelters and the conduct of the people. She sees families playing games, learning songs, even a group of people engaged in Bible reading and family prayers. I have had two letters from friends written from air-raid shelters, excellent letters, free from panic and full of meat.

["]I never knew there were so many gentlefolk in Bolton, more shame to me. I've kept to my own class, but now we are all Britons together,["] one old lady writes, after telling of her third bombing disaster. Hitler has united not only all Britons, but all the free people of the world.

A boy who left school here to enlist and is in an anti-aircraft squad, somewhere in England, writes, "We are no longer afraid of the German air raids, we think of them as thunder storms." He is hoping to be taken into the bomb-destroying force, he says.

Hitler would have foamed at the mouth if he could have been there the day after the big raid, market day, to see the farmers driving their cattle and sheep to market. The women gossiping over the sale of eggs, apples, plums and blackberries; the fishermen displaying their piles of fish and shrimps. There was an added warmth of friendliness in everyone's heart, because of the danger [they] had come through. If the Germans are expecting [their] morale to crack, they have a long road ahead of them.

They write well, these people who work and sleep under the German menace.

Into the stream of national literature there comes this season a tiny trickle of sweet water in the form of a modest little booklet told by Indian children and illustrated by a fourteen-year-old Indian boy. The little book is called *The Tale of the Nativity* and is written with a quaint charm and the stark simplicity of those who live in the open. The book comes from the Inkameep [Day] School in the Okanagan Valley in British Columbia and for it we are indebted to the understanding teacher, Anthony Walsh, who has patiently stimulated the artistic and dramatic talents of his pupils during the eight years he has been with them. In this world he has been helped by some public-spirited people who have now made the publication of the book possible.

Great poems came out of the last war and the first one that comes to mind is John McCrae's "In Flanders Fields." The McCrae family then collected and published their distinguished son's poems, [and] included only one reply of all the hundreds that were written and that was the one written by an eighteen-year-old Saskatchewan girl, Edna Jaques.

Edna Jaques is writing about this war in strangely moving little poems which reveal a tenderness and understanding that marks the true poet. Coming off the press this week, a slender volume of fifteen poems called *Britons Awake* comes from her pen and will be welcomed by her readers. At the price of a Christmas card, it should have a wide circulation.

It is strange about poetry and how blind we are to its value and how sublimely careless we are of our poets. The comforting legend is still believed that poets are fed by the ravens, as the Prophet Elijah, who dwelt by the brook Cherith, and therefore need no reward for their labours, beyond the rapture of pursuing. We should think of how poor life would be without these people who have the gift of making music with words.

Now, all of us, I believe, would like to pay tribute our beloved Queen [mother of Elizabeth II], who goes among her homeless people, with her charm, her grace, her sweet sympathy. But it was given to an American woman, Mary A. Winter, of Chicago, to frame in words, as simple as those found in a child's primer, the perfect tribute to this fair lady:

London Bridge is falling down,
My fair lady,
Be it said to your renown,
That you wore your gayest gown,
Your bravest smile, and stayed in town,
When London Bridge was falling down,
My fair lady!

"IT'S A GOOD THING FOR US TO READ BOOKS WRITTEN FROM THE OTHER SIDE OF THE WALL."

With Christmas coming around the corner and the need of Christmas spirit more imperative than ever in a world that seems in danger of forgetting what life was given to us for, I hope we can do something definite this year in the matter of Christmas giving.

Women are knitting and sewing for the people who need all the warmth, protection and comfort they can get. So let us count out bedroom slippers, pincushions, nightgowns, shopping bags and all that category of regular presents for the folks at home. Most of us have these, with extra ones still in their wrappings, in the lower bureau drawer.

This year, the need of our people is different. Our bodies are clothed, our dressing tables have a full supply of gadgets, but there is a clear and definite need for the things of the spirit.

I am always flattered when people give me books. There is something infinitely precious about books. They equalize life. They raise the standard of living like nothing else. We cannot all live in fine houses with broadloom carpets and pictures by the old masters, but we can all possess minted words of wisdom, mined from the greatest souls on Earth.

There is something pathetic in the falling market for books today when rare old volumes sell at the price of Penguin editions, but let us think of this in reverse and rejoice that more beautiful books are coming into the hands of real book lovers.

I have on my desk a hand-bound book printed on vellum, and I read on the fly leaf that forty-five years ago it was given to Beatrice May Howell, as a prize at Southfield, Dorchester. It is a book of poems dealing with Italian life.

Many of the poems in this book tell of the Italians' fight for freedom, bringing back to us, in these days of frantic boastings and treacherous "stabs in the back," the fact that the Italians have been a gentle people, who read poetry and fairy tales and love music and who have, until recent years, occupied an honoured place in the Family of Nations.

I have just read a modern book, *The Heart of a Child,* by Phyllis Bottome, which is the story of a little German boy and his dog, who lived and suffered in the hard days of starvation following the last war. The peasants of Feldmuss, a little village in the high mountains, believed that the English were savage and cruel and were the cause of all their miseries, but at the end of the war, the Society of Friends mysteriously appeared with their hands full of gifts and the word went out through the village that a Christmas party would be given to all the children.

Karl, the hero of the story, who had stolen money from the church to save the life of his dog, Rolf, was torn with fear and suspicion. He was afraid to take his young brothers and sisters to the English women's party. He knew the English had great guns of destruction and was afraid that this party was nothing but a blind. However, the kind faces of the English women and the prospect of something to eat overcame his fears, and Karl and his nine brothers and sisters went to the party, and what a party it was!

The high point of the proceedings came when a Christmas tree blazed at them out of the dark and at the foot there lay the Holy Child, in His manger cradle with Mary in her blue cloak beside Him and Joseph standing guard. Warmed and fed in body and mind, the little boy went to the church before going home and made his peace with God, restoring the money to the poor box, and offered a prayer:

"Please God forgive the English if they need it and thank you for sending them and a Merry Christmas to you and me and Rolf."

It's a good thing for us to read books written from the other side of the wall. Books are the best ambassadors. They bind us to our fellow man more securely than treaties. The burning of the books in Germany was a crime against all humanity, a symbolic act, which shows that the mind and soul of their people has been cut off from human relationships with the other people of the world for the purpose of starving them into spiritual servility and mental death.

We wouldn't burn books here in Canada. We are too civilized for that. But let us take care that we do not ignore them. The results are not dissimilar. We relate with pride that the Bible is the best-selling book in the world, but a Bible on a shelf is just a piece of merchandise, as sterile as a china egg.

Last year, when we read of the Finnish people dropping New Testaments on their enemies, it came as a challenge to many of us. What are we doing to spread the Gospel even among our friends?

iv. Toward Equality

Nellie McClung devoted *much of her life to the fight for women's equality in Canada. From her early days of attending WCTU meetings with her future mother-in-law, Annie McClung, to the historic formation of the Famous Five, Nellie was a trailblazer who never stopped caring about women's issues. By the time Nellie moved to Vancouver Island and began writing her column, in 1936, most Canadian women could vote in federal and provincial elections. Notably, of course, this right was not extended to Indigenous people, who did not gain full voting rights until 1960. As well, Canadians of Chinese, Japanese, and Indian descent were not granted the right to vote until 1947 (for Chinese and Indo-Canadians) and 1948 (for Japanese Canadians). In Quebec, women (who did not fall under the aforementioned groups) gained the right to vote in provincial elections in 1940, considerably later than the other provinces. The landmark personhood case launched by the Famous Five in 1927 was decided in 1929, when women (again, not all women, but most women in Canada) were eligible to become members of the Senate—though such an appointment was not made until 1974.*

Although the system was far from perfect, and gender inequality is ongoing, no one can deny that a great deal of progress occurred between 1916 and 1929, and that Nellie McClung was an influential figure in that period of change. Yet Nellie herself was not satisfied, and she continued to write about women's issues—sometimes critically—well into her sixties. Her feminism was deeply rooted in her Christian beliefs and her unwavering belief in Christian democracy. The following columns begin with a look back at the great achievements of the Famous Five and go on to address some of Nellie's disappointments with the progression of the movement since then.

D & J TRUMBLEY

"THIS WAS EVERY WOMAN'S CONCERN."

Everything in life is a circle. There are no sharp corners. Cause and effect run together all the way. The event that took place a week ago in Ottawa, when a plaque was unveiled commemorating the decision of the Privy Council that women are persons, was a culmination of something that began twenty years ago in the Women's Court in Edmonton.

Magistrate Emily Murphy had given a decision that enraged one of the lawyers. His client had been given a heavy penalty. The lawyer assailed the decision on the ground that Murphy's appointment to the position of magistrate was illegal, for women were not persons under the British common law.

Murphy, being a wise woman, looked carefully into the matter. She often said that one must never belittle the argument of the opponent. She read the famous case of Charlton vs. Ling of 1868 and its ruling: "Women are not persons in matters of rights and privileges, but they are persons in matters of pains and penalties."

The law had not been rescinded, and there was no doubt that it was still valid, though public opinion had rendered it obsolete. Murphy, as well as some others of us, had interviewed honourable members at Ottawa from time to time on the matter of appointing women to the Senate and we had received the same reply: The

British North America Act had made no provision for women, and the members feared that women could not be appointed to the Senate until this great foundation of our liberties was amended, and that would take time and careful thought.

The clause in the British North America Act dealing with the Senate appointments reads as follows: "Properly qualified persons may from time to time be summoned to the Senate."

And always there arose that spectre: Women were not persons under the common law of England.

Murphy, whose business it was to know the law, believed that there was a way of getting this matter cleared up. We would ask the Parliament of Canada for an interpretation of this clause. Any five British subjects, of the full age of twenty-one, could petition Parliament for an interpretation of any act.

So one day, near the end of August in 1927, we gathered at Murphy's home in South Edmonton. It was a perfect day in harvest time. Blue haze lay on the horizon. Wheat fields, now dotted with stooks, were waiting for the threshing machine. Bees droned in the delphiniums and roses. We sat on her verandah and talked the afternoon away. Then we put our names to the petition and it was sent to Ottawa.

In November, the Department of Justice referred the matter to the Supreme Court of Canada. But they did not render a decision until April 24, 1928, and then it came as a shattering blow to our hopes.

In the opinion of the Supreme Court of Canada, women were not persons!

Four out of the five judges based their judgment on the common-law disability of women to hold public office, and the other one believed the word "person" in the BNA Act meant male person, because the framers of the act had only men in mind when the clause was written.

We met again, this time in Calgary, and contemplated our defeat. Murphy was still undaunted. We would appeal the Supreme Court decision. We would send our petition to the Privy Council.

We asked her what we would use for money. Lawyers' fees, we knew, were staggering. When a lawyer is writing his fees for a service of this kind, his hand often slips. Murphy said she would write to the prime minister. Perhaps he could devise a way. This was every woman's concern and she was sure that the government would be glad to have it settled. The letter was written and we had a prompt reply.

On October 18, 1929, the newspapers carried the black headline, "Privy Council Declares Women Are Persons."

The Lord Chancellor had given the decision and it was so simple and plain that we wonder now why we did not think of it ourselves. Lord Sankey found the solution in the British North America Act itself, under two headings:

First: There are clauses in the act where the word "male" persons is used, which leads one to believe that "person" must mean male and female person.

Second: There is one clause in the act where the word "person" must mean male and female. It is Clause 133, which provides that either the French or English language may be used by any person in any court established under this act. The word "person" must include women, as it is inconceivable that this privilege was given to men only.

There were other reasons given in His Lordship's fourteen-page judgment, but that was the one that closed the debate.

Now it is all over. The circle is complete. The Business and Professional Women of Canada have graciously placed a memorial plaque in the lobby of the Senate, House of Parliament, Ottawa, to mark this event. The speeches will be over when this appears in print.

There are only two of us left now of the five, and we feel, as did Mrs. Edwards and Mrs. McKinney, that we, like all the women of Canada, are indebted to Emily F. Murphy for this definite, clear-cut victory, which has clarified the position of women in the whole British Empire.

"SO, WHAT MORE DO THEY WANT?"

> JUNE 11, 1938

What is the matter with them? What makes them discontented? Isn't it true that they do 75 percent of all the purchasing of consumer goods and are the beneficiaries in 80 percent of all insurance policies and in 70 percent of all estates left by men?

They own property, bank stock and bonds out of all proportion to their earnings. Isn't it true that advertisers direct their efforts to catch the eyes of women; that houses are built to please them; that clothes are designed for them; wild animals are slain to provide them with furs to keep them warm and make them beautiful; that precious stones are mined and cut and polished for their delight; magazines and books are written for them; and to complete the recital of their good fortune, statistics tell us they live longer than men?

So, what more do they want?

They have money, security, care, beauty [and] long life and yet it is these women who throng the waiting rooms in doctors' offices and wait in queues to have their fortunes told. Have women any special cause for grief and discontent?

Undoubtedly they have lost part of their work. But much of that they were glad to lose. What sound is more cheerful than the mellow rhythm of an electric washer? Machinery has lifted the burden of housework. Factories have taken over the dressmaking and canning. Women have emerged from the kitchen and have now become the leisured class. They have time to play golf, belong to clubs, study languages and do social services work, and some of them do these things.

But life has taken a queer turn on the women whose work lies outside the home. Many new occupations were opened to women during the war, and these were efficiently filled, with the result that women were no longer wanted. It was nobody's fault. Naturally, men wanted their jobs back and the women were thrown out. Since then, women who occupy well-paid positions are under suspicion. There is little chance of promotion. This is still a man's world.

Germany and Italy have done what some of our people would like to do. They have been ruthless and thorough and did not argue. The women have been sent back to the kitchen and told that their reason for existence is the bearing of soldiers for their country.

When women were given the vote in 1916–17 on the North American continent, we did not foresee these happenings. We believed that enfranchisement meant emancipation. We spoke glibly of freedom. We were obsessed with the belief that we could cleanse and purify the world by law. We said women were naturally lovers of peace and purity, temperance and justice.

There never has been a campaign like the Suffrage campaign. It was a clear-cut issue. You were either with us or against us. We had all the arguments and, mixed with our zeal for public righteousness, there was a definite content of animosity for those who opposed us.

We did not think much of them. We saw them as obstacles to be removed. The second verse of the national anthem (the one that is left out now) was our prayer: "Scatter our enemies—and make them fall. Confound their politics, frustrate their knavish tricks."

We rejoiced over their discomfiture when victory came to us. But when all was over and the smoke of battle cleared away, something happened to us. Our forces, so well organized for the campaign, began to dwindle. We had no constructive program for making a new world. Even the Church did not see that there was a great volume of power ready to be used. Indeed, the hostility of certain sections of the Church to women's advancement drove many women away from religious organizations.

So the enfranchised women drifted. Many are still drifting. Material things will never satisfy either men or women. Every one of us, in our low moments, have wished they could. Who has not envied the cows in the meadow, the ducks on the pond? Wishing for that dreamless contentment which is bounded by food and shelter and sleep!

But we knew better. We knew that man cannot live by bread alone—and not even by bread and science. We knew all the time that even philosophy solves no problems, for it does not change the heart. All these may show us what we ought to do but they will not give us the power to do it. That takes something deeper. We knew that but we did not do anything about it.

Harvard University recently celebrated its three hundredth anniversary and in its celebration this tragic condition was admitted. Individuals are weaker and less happy now than they were. Men live longer but are more at war with themselves than ever. Nations are more liable to internal strife and the world is further from international peace! Our spiritual forces have not been called out.

So here is the situation. Philosophy has explained the world. We know why life goes stale; we know why people end their lives; we know about repressions and frustrations and moral breakdowns. It is not enough to be able to explain things. We must cure them. We must turn sorrow into joy. We must turn enemies into friends.

"IT IS NO DISGRACE TO BE 'LADYLIKE.'"

> NOVEMBER 16, 1940

When Hitler made the boast that after he had conquered Europe he would not need to use arms against the United States, for he would have enough people in the United States to colonize it, many of us dismissed this as another one of his foolish boasts.

But as time rolls on and we see and read what is coming over to us from some of the internationally known writers of the United States, we begin to see that the German dictator had some grounds for hope.

We all know that Hitler eradicated two factors from German life early in his rule, the influence of women and the church in all its forms. For these he had a fiery hatred that can easily be understood—he wanted no softness in his people, no mercy, no charity, no brotherly love, no conscience. So he dismissed women from public offices, drove them to working in the fields or in the homes, insisted on an increased birthrate, and as far as he was able, closed the churches and imprisoned or shot the priests and pastors who dared to resist him.

Now we find that Hitler has his disciples on this side of the Atlantic and naturally we are worried over this. Not only should women be worried, but all thinking people.

Channing Pollock, well-known literary critic and dramatist, writes in the October *Readers' Digest* an article entitled "Why I Do Not Go to Church," as bitter and unfair an attack as only a clever man could devise. He assails the church from many angles.

The ministers, he says, "dwelling in ivory towers, know nothing of life. They have nothing to say and must say it twice on Sunday." He says their sermons, "as reported in the newspapers," show superficial thinking, limited experience and pious platitudes.

He says the cost of the ornate church structures might better have been used to feed thousands of starved minds, which certainly has a familiar sound. ("Should not this have been sold and given to the poor?")

Now it is not my intention to fill this column with a defence of the church, though I could do this with a good heart. I have listened many times to long-distance selfish critics, who never go near a church, or give a dollar to its support, who base their observations on "newspaper reports," which naturally are brief and sketchy, and yet feel competent to attack the self-sacrificing ministers and people who carry on day by day, teaching in Sunday schools, welcoming strangers, guiding young people, and giving a Gospel message here and in other lands.

I think of the boys' and girls' camps, the fresh-air camps, where tired women and sick children are given a holiday; the free libraries, reading rooms, gymnasiums.

But greater than all these is the teaching of the church. That is the mission of the church—to be a light in the darkness. And it is just that. Boys and girls are taught in the church to know right from wrong, to have a sense of God's nearness and recognize temptation and know how to meet it. This is more than feeding the hungry and clothing the naked.

The lesson of this tragic hour is plain. The last stand of democracy is the fortified hearts of its people, and the human heart is fortified against fear, and death, when it trusts in God. Christ came to Earth to bring that message. He died for it, so sure He was that His message would redeem the world, and so it will.

His disciples were ordinary men, full of fear and self-seeking, but when they saw His resurrection, they became strong and fearless. They knew that nothing mattered but the truth.

That is the teaching of the Church of Christ and we must be faithful to it. It is the hope of the world.

The church does make demands on its people, which lazy and indifferent people are loath to meet. So they make excuses for themselves. They do not honestly say: "I'm too lazy to go to church— I want to amuse myself on Sundays. I don't care what happens to the young people—let them run amok—they'll learn by experience. It's not my responsibility, anyway."

People of this cast of thought will be delighted with Channing Pollock's reasons for not going to church. Here is comfort and exoneration. Let me quote again from Pollock:

"We find the kind of religion offered in churches to be the preservation of symbols, doctrines and a philosophy largely without meaning in our modern world . . . underpaid and underprivileged persons, given a circumscribed education, turned loose without taste or opportunity for further development . . . Such men cannot command the respect of their communities . . . Why should you or I waste an hour on half-baked social theories that might be spent with Herbert Spenser [sic] or poor Ortega y Gasset?"

Is this what Hitler meant when he spoke of colonization?

The "colonization" goes on in another direction, too, equally subtle and mischievous.

As good a magazine as *Harper's* carried an article last month blaming women's influence in America for the country's unpreparedness. That's a good one. The writer says that somewhere between 1914 and 1940, both Britain and France became ladylike. It is no disgrace to be "ladylike," though the word here is intended to convey a picture of a timid old lady who wears frilled petticoats and who screams when she sees a mouse.

Well, maybe she did in peacetime but now that same old lady in England or Scotland has probably extinguished incendiary bombs that fell in her room and torn up her petticoats to staunch the blood of her countrymen. I do not think that much criticism can be directed against the women of Britain at this moment, on any count. Of course, I know it's wonderful to have someone to blame.

There are two ways of taking unfair criticism. One is to mull over it, get hot about it, rehearse imaginary conversations with the critics and otherwise waste the energy needed in our work.

The other way is to search for any word of truth that may be buried in the trash. We are the church. If it is impotent, it is because we are indifferent. The church has workers and well-wishers. More well-wishers than workers.

Its efficiency could be doubled now if the well-wishers would suddenly awaken to its importance. It is not just another Good Cause, to which five dollars is given when the collectors call. The church is a great service station on life's hard road. It is a lighthouse on a stormy sea. The enemies of humanity consider it a military objective.

v. Second World War

From the start *of the Second World War until 1943, Nellie McClung wrote some of her most forceful and overtly political columns. Although she continued to weave in references to lighter topics such as gardening and holidays, there was an underlying determination to motivate her readers to care about state of the country and the world as a whole. Some columns seem uncharacteristically grim, while her optimism shines in others. Whatever her tone, Nellie wrote knowledgeably and eloquently about world events, and her insights are still fascinating to read. In the following columns she tackled everything from the Soviet invasion of Finland to the Red Cross to the European refugee crisis. As always, she was motivated by her faith in her religion and her unwavering belief in a just society.*

In November 1940, Nellie suffered a heart attack while attending a CBC Board of Directors meeting. Her doctors ordered her to scale back her activities and she did, as far as she was able to without losing her sense of herself as a highly capable and productive woman. She resigned her directorship with the CBC, though in August 1943 she was well enough to host her fellow members of the board when they met in Victoria. That was the year she stopped writing her weekly newspaper column, but she kept up with correspondence that she herself described as "voluminous," as well as other newspaper articles and pieces for magazines.

140

"EVERY FREE NATION, EVERY NATION WHICH VALUES FREEDOM, WILL EVER BE INDEBTED TO THESE STOUT-HEARTED PEOPLE."

> JANUARY 20, 1940

When a radio commentator, a few mornings ago, speaking from Helsingfors [Helsinki], wanted to make his listeners understand the Finns, he said: "They are just like ourselves. They eat bacon and eggs for breakfast and drink coffee and look like the folks of Emporia, Kansas."

So they do. And we flatter ourselves here in Canada that we have many points of similarity with this gallant country, too, whose name is now on everyone's lips.

Russia, in her attempt to blot out her independent little neighbour, to reduce its cities to darkness and ashes, and its people to serfdom, has really crowned Finland with immortality. No matter what happens, one thing is certain: Every free nation, every nation which values freedom, will ever be indebted to these stout-hearted people. Their fame will never die, unless all the lamps of liberty are blown out!

Finland is the most northerly civilized country in the world, part of its territory running into the Arctic Circle. In spite of its northerly situation, its climate is no colder that our own Manitoba and Saskatchewan. January and February are the coldest months.

July is the hottest month, and May is the time of sowing. Helsingfors has a winter climate that closely resembles that of Halifax.

The sea, which is her chief means of communications with the outside world, freezes over almost every winter, and strength and foresight have been developed because of this isolation.

Finland has also had to solve a language problem more complicated than ours. Until 1809, Finland had lived under the rule of Sweden, and Swedish had become the language of the educated class. At that date Finland fell under the power of Russia and the fate of the Finnish language seemed certain. It was spoken only by the working people, on the farms and in the woods.

But in the hearts of the leaders, even though they spoke Swedish, burned a great patriotic zeal. They knew that Finnish independence was closely bound up with the Finnish language and so began an agitation in favour of the native tongue.

One of these was the great [Hannes] Snellman, a journalist who imbued the press of the country with a keen sense of nationalism, and a great intellectual revival began, which culminated in Finland's victory twenty years ago. The struggle lasted more than a hundred years, and now Finnish education commands the admiration of the world; but it was not until 1883 that the Finnish language was formally adopted as the medium for law courts and public offices.

The presence of an outside power, that of Russia, drew the Swedish and Finnish elements of the country together and caused them to make a sane and peaceful settlement of this grave question of language. They were wise enough to see that a difference in language did not necessarily mean antagonism of thought, and when the victory came in 1919, the new constitution expressly recognized the existence of two national languages, and assured to the Swedish minority complete linguistic equality.

Finland has never been rich in material things, but they had had great regard for the things of the spirit. No boy or girl is allowed to suffer from the carelessness of parents in matters of education. "Continuation" schools follow the child into maturity. If an employer engages an illiterate person, he must allow time off for schooling.

All this exacting care has resulted in Finland having the lowest illiteracy percentage in the world. Finland was one of the first countries to give women equality before the law. We received our bill of rights in Canada in 1917—Finnish women were enfranchised eleven years previously.

Finnish women have many societies, including the YWCA and the National Council of Women, both affiliated with the international bodies, and one organization called the Lotta Svärd, which only exists in Finland. It is a women's unit of defence, which gives assistance in both peace and wartime to the Defence Corps. They wear a grey uniform and were organized in 1919. The "Lottas," as they are called, give assistance in the matters of food, clothing [and] hospital care and particularly in the development of patriotic sentiment. In wartime they follow the army, doing everything except the actual fighting.

It has not happened by chance that the Finnish army has outwitted the Russians. It is revealing to read of their military education. There is no boredom in their training. The soldiers' day begins at 5:00 a.m. and ends at 10:00 at night. Five or six hours are spent out of doors. The remainder of the time is spent in indoor studies. There are lectures given on Finnish history, literature, sociology and natural science. Libraries exist in every garrison centre. There are also "Soldiers Homes," maintained by the self-sacrificing zeal of the civil population, especially the women.

When freedom was won in 1919, they evidently had no illusions on the subject of permanent peace. I quote from one of their political writers a paragraph written at that time: "Owing to the geographical position of our country, few generations of Finns have reached the peace of the grave without experiencing in their own persons the hardships of war. Having at long last attained our hearts' desire, political independence, our most earnest wish is now to be allowed to enjoy the blessings of peaceful progress, protected by our own national defence force. The soldiers of Finland are deeply conscious of their high duty as the invincible defenders of an independent realm, to maintain its inviolability against all foes. When the moment of danger comes, they will gloriously answer the call. This is a sacred obligation imposed upon them by the unstained martial reputation of their forefathers; they have to maintain and defend western civilization, the cultural achievements and the political independence of the Republic of Finland."

The Russians are fighting because they are ordered to fight. Naturally a peaceable people, with no bitterness in their hearts, they hate this senseless campaign against their inoffensive neighbours. The Finns are fighting for the right of every free people to live, and they know it. They are upheld by a good conscience, void of offence against all men. No wonder their eyes are keen, and their aim sure!

"A BOY OF THE FARM WHO WOULD HAVE
BEEN A PRODUCER, A BUILDER, A SOWER OF CROPS."

> JANUARY 27, 1940

War is not only a waste of things we can see and touch, but makes heavy inroads on the invisible and intangible things of the spirit. I saw a mother saying goodbye to a red-cheeked, downy-faced boy, to whom she had given much love and care. Just in that one fleeting glance I could see that she had made a good job and had produced a kind, generous, high-minded lad, who believes in God and in humanity and who is now going out to fight for his country with every nerve in his body quivering with a sense of high adventure. A boy of the farm who would have been a producer, a builder, a sower of crops.

Now the chances are he will do none of these things. All his life is changed. I know what she meant when she said goodbye to him. It was more than goodbye. It was goodbye forever. She knew it, too, and that's why I tried to comfort her when she said, "Even if he comes back, he will never be the same."

War is an ugly thing. No one tries to glorify it now. But there are some things uglier. Slavery, for instance. I would like to be an out-and-out pacifist. I envy the Quakers who go about doing good, in and out of belligerent countries, welcome everywhere with their quiet faces, compassionate eyes, hands of healing and words of hope.

But the Quakers, I am afraid, even if their numbers were multiplied a hundredfold, could not bring peace to troubled Europe. Not now. It's too late. So the downy-faced boys, who kept pets and collected stamps and went hiking on Saturday, have to be turned into fighting men. Fire has to be fought with fire, force with force. It is a hard remedy, involving unspeakable horror and waste. No one likes it, but what else can we do?

If we were dealing with reasonable people, we could make a bargain. No one can say that Neville Chamberlain did not try to "neighbour" with the German chancellor.

Since the war, some new words have come into our vocabulary —appeasement and encirclement and now a still newer one, *lebensraum*, which means "living space." This is the word Hitler used to describe the need of the German people, who are, he says, choking and smothering for space. So he proceeds to tear other people up by the roots, rifling their treasures, bombing their churches and hospitals, beating and robbing them, throwing them out to wander and die, to make room for the German people. Doing all this with no more compunction than the pioneers of Ontario [who] cut down trees to make way for their fields of wheat and oats.

It is not living space he wants; it is power.

The old Germany, prior to 1914, was slowly but surely conquering the world by the excellence of its goods and services. "Made in Germany" was an honourable phrase. German vessels were welcome in every port. Her universities were the ambition of students all over the world. Her sanitoria were full of people from other countries. "Educated in Germany" was a proud boast.

German hotels, their excellent cooking, their friendliness, thrift, their thoroughness, their clean streets, their system of education—these were all held up as examples to us. People of my generation were brought up with admiration for Germany.

Now east and west, and north and south, Germany has not a friend, except one doubtful and uncertain country that is causing her bitter embarrassment and the loss of her only other ally. The small nations of Europe are trembling in their shoes. There is not one of them that would not rather be dead than fall into the hands of Germany. War is waste, bitter waste, but not such a soul-destroying waste as government by violence and robbery.

We have learned something from the last war. The conservation of men, the policy of waiting, the elimination of profit. These are the concrete lessons that we have learned.

Spiritually, we have learned more. We know now that men's minds must change if we are ever to have peace. The old selfishness and pride of race and clan have to give way. England, France and the United States must show the way to a higher level of living, which is just so many words strung together unless those who write and read these words are filled with that new spirit. It begins today, at home, at this hour and is an intensely practical thing.

When peace comes, that spirit must be manifest or we will do no better than we did before and our grandchildren will have to fight another war. We are our brother's keeper whether we like it or not, and if there is oppression and injustice in one part of the world, our own part of the world, however remote, will sooner or later be infected.

The world is one neighbourhood now. That is the penalty we pay for our advancement in science, invention, rapid transit, easy communication. We have to accept life as it is now. The day of indifference is over. People can no longer take refuge behind a hedge of nationalism. Our concern now is to win the war, dethrone the gods of violence and then make a just peace on the foundation of human brotherhood. The path ahead of us is rough, but plain.

"WHO KNOWS WHAT THIS YEAR'S GROWTH MAY BE?"

No matter how tangled any thread is, if we look at a small enough part of it, it seems to lie straight. So it is in life.

I am going out to look at such a small area of life today that there will be no room left for tangles. The day is fair and the countryside lies about me, green and beautiful. White clouds are piling up in cathedral mountains beyond San Juan Island and one boat with an orange sail rides on the gentle waves of the straits.

I have a flower and shrub catalogue with me and I am going to sit on a log and read it from end to end and forget the world. Real flowers are never as lovely as their pictures in the catalogue, but I put that thought away as a suggestion of evil. Who knows what this year's growth may be?

I have been reading an article in *The Listener*, by Denis Saurat, about French peasants. He says if you took money away from them it would make no difference in their lives. They would eat the same things from their land, do the same work with their cows and horses. Their real wealth is in their grass, pigs, horses.

That's one thing the war is doing for us. We are learning something about our brave allies! Now that England and France are doing their buying as well as their fighting as one nation, here in Canada we may yet have French taught in our schools and, in one

149

generation, we may become truly bilingual, and that would help us on our way to being a great nation.

Now, I hear, the French are asked by the people of Spain to give back the refugee children they took in during the war in Spain, and they are refusing. They are too fond of the little strangers to part with them and no doubt the boys and girls are useful now!

There! I am taking in too large a slice of life and must get back to the safe shelter of the catalogue.

I will look at the shrubs. We have a place at the north of the house where no flower seems happy, and this year we are going to put in shrubs. I read about flowering cherries and here are their pictures! The best collection may now be seen in Washington, DC, where the magnificent gift of the Japanese government is in full bloom.

In these hard, sorrowful days when we cannot sleep at night for thinking of the world's trouble, we must sweeten our hearts with simple things like the smell of violets in the rain and the sight of crimson berries which shine through the fog, for these are more than merely vegetable growth that can be resolved into their components parts of chlorophyll and pigment—they are tokens and signs sent to us, as the rainbow was to Noah and his family, to assure us that God has not forgotten the world.

"THAT CRY FOR LEADERS IS AN OLD EXCUSE. WHAT WE NEED TODAY ARE FOLLOWERS."

> MARCH 16, 1940

A big, throaty voice was calling on the radio for leaders. Leaders like Joshua, Moses and Amos! Leaders like Lincoln and Wilberforce, who would flash a message, meteor-like across the sky! He said, "Humanity is stalled on life's highway for lack of leaders." I knew what I wanted to say. It is not leaders we need— we have always had leaders. We all know enough, at least we know more than we are using, and so perhaps the best way to increase our knowledge is to put into practice what we already know.

"Words," I said to myself, quoting an old proverb, "are the daughters of Earth but deeds are the sons of Heaven."

That cry for leaders is an old excuse. What we need today are followers. Someone who will work without being told just what to do. Someone who will work continuously and not sit back after their first effort waiting to be thanked or reported or complimented.

We have all the elements of successful living in Canada. We have freedom of speech, assembly and thought. We are not only literate, we are intelligent. We have organizations of which we are proud. We have auxiliaries to almost everything.

Even so, there are men and women who have not yet found themselves. They go on their way, untouched by the turmoil around them, feeling no responsibility for the problems of their fellow men.

They are not hard of heart or dull of mind. They are merely detached and take the spectator attitude to everything. If we could ever get through to people of this class, they would release a great new force for the building of citizenship here in Canada.

The war has complicated all our problems. We had a full allotment of problems prior to September 1939. We still have these and a complete set of new ones. If they could only be solved by oratory, resolutions and letters to the paper, all would be well, but unfortunately these can only be solved by hard thinking and patient and enduring toil.

We have many new people in Canada today, people who are here because of conditions in Europe. They are naturally distraught, homesick, unsettled and lonely. They need friends more than anything in the world. If we reach out to them and draw them into our society, Canada will be infinitely richer for their presence.

This type of friendship takes time and energy, tact and understanding. And we still have our problems of unemployment. One person in every twenty is dependent on the other nineteen. And yet the Minister of Transport has recently said that there may soon be a labour shortage in Canada. He means, of course, a shortage of trained labour.

We have never exercised our fullest energy in this matter of finding work for our own people, nor have we exercised our best efforts to train people. We all know people who hold on to jobs long after the time when they should retire and give the younger ones a chance. We all know people who are well able to employ labour and yet are not doing it.

Why do people hold so tightly to this elusive thing called money? Are we allowing our desire for security to blind us to the dangers about us? It is safer to put money in a new house or a new room on the old house than to leave it lying in the bank.

That is what we mean when we speak of houses and lands as "real estate." A house may depreciate by wind and weather, but money depreciates still faster by the chill winds of depression, and depressions always follow war.

There is a higher motive, too, than this selfish one. Our people are our glory and our wealth. The very essence of democracy and Christianity lies in the value of the individual. Germany and Russia stand convicted before the whole world in their disregard for human life. They sacrifice human beings without mercy, turning back the clock of civilization to the Dark Ages.

We know we must help our own people. "Unless you bring your brother with you, you shall not see my face." That is what Joseph said when talking to his brothers who came to Egypt to buy corn. In saying this he uttered an unalterable truth. In a Christian democracy, no one can be allowed to grow bitter in idleness. The success of a democracy depends on the individual.

There never was a time when people were thinking so earnestly of this and looking so eagerly for channels through which their energy can flow. It all becomes very simple, if we are each willing to do the thing which lies nearest to our hands, however humble that may be.

A young man called at a house in a western city, asking for work. He was neatly dressed, well-spoken and desperately anxious to earn money. The first impulse of the lady of the house was to tell him she had no chores to be done but, fortunately, she was touched by the eagerness of his manner and set him to wash her car.

There were some apples in a box in the garage which needed to be picked over and he asked if he might do this. She found out that he had a wife and two children, and the more she talked to him the more she became interested in his case. She took his address and the next day went to see his family and found a case of dire poverty.

A month-old baby was sleeping in a cardboard carton, wrapped in a blanket and nothing else. There was no bed in the house and very little food, but the people were intelligent and hopeful. Their new friend, who happened to be a teacher, gave them something for their immediate needs and told her pupils about them.

The results have been interesting. The family has been established in a better house—the children are now clothed—the man has been given work and the pupils of this Grade Four [class] have learned something about social responsibility. All because the teacher was ready to do what came her way.

The theorists will cry out that charity is not a remedy, but if we can multiply charity over and over, it will hasten the remedy. Interested people, if we have enough of them, will provide a remedy for anything.

No one need be idle these days if they have in their heart the faintest glimmering of a desire to help their country. Many women find their place in doing war work, looking after the welfare of soldiers.

In one city, eight women met at a luncheon three months ago and talked about the need for recreation in some place where the soldiers could bring their women friends—where they could read and write and have refreshments at cost. There were eight young women at the luncheon—not one of them either rich or socially prominent, but they had brains and energy and they were in earnest.

Now the "Georgia Dugout" in Vancouver is open every day in the week for the members of the Armed Forces and their friends, and there are three hundred women enrolled as voluntary workers. There is an orchestra, a dancing floor, a writing room, a library. More than this, there is good talk and fellowship over the tea tables.

No, it is not a matter of leadership; it is a question of who is willing to work. Who will knit for a soldier when they would rather be making something for themselves? Who will hunt out the lonely ones who live on the other side of the tracks? Who will go down back streets looking for some newcomer in a rooming house who may be homesick and discouraged? Who will upset the even tenor of a busy life to befriend the needy?

The various elements in our country are like the stones needed for a building. They are strong, beautiful, durable. But they cannot be held together without cement, and this social cement is the thousand little acts of understanding of which we are capable—insignificant taken singly but mighty in their accumulation for the up-building of our nation.

"CANADIANS, I BELIEVE, ARE BEGINNING TO STIR IN THEIR SLEEP."

> APRIL 13, 1940

The bright sun of spring shows up the dust of winter in the curtains, the faded places on the wallpaper, the finger marks on the windows, the cobwebs in the corners, and a fiery urge to clean and sweep and paint and burn fills the heart of women everywhere. Soon the clotheslines will be full of blankets rippling in the breeze, and the sound of the vacuum cleaner will be heard in the land. It is not so dramatic as the old carpet beater, but more effective.

When this appears in print, spring will be rolling into action all across the country, and no more heartening time can ever come than these first bright days when the blue anemone decks the headlands and the meadow lark pipes his joyous song from fence post and poplar tree. The cattle on the meadows lift their heads and listen and know that the time of grass has come.

There will be a tremendous amount of energy released this year in the great cleaning and a great planting, for the darkening skies in Europe and anxiety at home will drive people into action. It shows already in the increased demand for bulbs and seeds and garden tools.

This great creative urge, properly directed, could beautify the countryside and lift the faces of our little towns and villages. At this

155

in-between season, the little places, stripped of the kindly mantle of snow, under which all deformities were hidden, appear sad and depressed in the merciless April sunshine. Many of them look like motherless children with dirty faces, matted hair and fallen stockings. Papers blow down lanes and catch in fences; blinds are crooked and gates sag on broken hinges.

Much of this will be changed when the women's institutes go into action, but unfortunately there are no organized bands of women in many of these districts. Only one-tenth of the women in Canada belong to any organization.

But perhaps this year there will come a stirring of civic pride, and Canada will get ready for company. There will be a tourist movement this year greater than we have ever seen, and preparations for this should begin now.

We could make our highways beautiful with annuals—the free bloomers, nasturtiums, bachelors' buttons, marigolds. School grounds, church grounds, community halls could all be made more attractive with a bit of care.

Switzerland is not a rich country, but it attracts the tourists by its thrift and beauty. Every little corner bears its contribution of colour and fragrance, for the people have a love for flowers not only in their own gardens but beyond. The apple trees along the roads in France, whose fruit is free to any who wish to pick it, is another indication of people's thrift and forethought. (Speaking of apples, I notice in an Edmonton paper the suggestion that each schoolchild be given an apple a day to use up our surplus.)

There is a little town in Texas called Lubbock, which for ten years has held the prize for the cleanest town in the state. There is not one millionaire in Lubbock, yet all are prosperous. People who go there stay. In the last three years nearly two thousand new houses have been built. It has the lowest tax rate in the state, and the lowest electric rating from its own plant. The civic pride of the people has brought all this to pass.

Canadians, I believe, are beginning to stir in their sleep, conscious of a new destiny. I remember twenty-five years ago hearing

Mrs. Emily Murphy in an Empire Day address say that some day Ottawa might become the heart of the British Empire. *The New York Times* has put it this way: "One thing is already certain, Canada will become a more important part of the Empire than seemed likely only a few short years ago. Her selection for, and adoption of the great British Commonwealth air-training system, upon which the outcome of the whole war may depend, ensures that. She is already the link between the old and the new world of Anglo-Saxon civilization. She may conceivably become its heart."

Whether or not we are capable to assume this high calling in a despairing world does not depend on our money, our wheat or our minerals. It depends on our spirit.

Last month, at the great missionary congress held in New York, a radio message was received from Holland's queen in which she voiced the hope that is in many hearts, that out of this confusion may come the still small voice of Faith which will guide us all into better ways.

"May mankind learn to look through the eyes of Christ," said the Netherlands queen, "and by doing so overcome all ideas, sentiments and conditions that keep men apart."

Technically, millions of people on this continent subscribe to this sentiment. We sing it in our hymns. We read it in our poetry. We even pray it in our prayers. A few days ago we listened to the Easter story. We heard the bells and thought about the risen Lord, and in our hearts we knew that miracles could happen.

Christmas and Easter are times of refreshing, when something not of Earth flows into our hearts to make us conscious of another and a better world; not far away beyond the skies, but within us now, an invisible kingdom of the Spirit, in which all things are possible.

As I write this, it seems true. It is real and satisfying to me at this moment. But knowing what I do of life and the deflections of the human heart, its ebb and flow, the ecstasies of the mountain-top, the gloom of the valley, I know we must do something if we are to hold the glow in our hearts which Easter and the budding trees have brought.

So I went out and moved a peony into a better place. It was shaded by a laurel bush and did not do well last year. I have it in the sunshine now, where it will have a chance to grow and bloom.

I wish every child whose little life is darkened could get a change for growth like this. I am thinking now of the 9,400 little refugees in England looking to Canada for homes—little orphans of the storm, frightened little things whose eyes are full of fear. Canada could take them, feed them, clothe them, love them.

"IS IT ENOUGH TO BIND WOUNDS AND OUTFIT THE FIGHTING MEN—IF THEY ARE THEREBY MERELY ENABLED TO FIGHT AGAIN?"

> MAY 4, 1940

"The Red Cross is one of the few humanitarian ideas that has ever become a reality. Above the barbarism of our times, it stands out as a great monument to the nineteenth century."

This is a sentence from the book called *Dunant: The Story of the Red Cross*, which was written two years ago by Martin Gumpert and which has a heightened interest for us now.

The Red Cross came into being by the gigantic efforts of a man called Henri Dunant, a native of Geneva, who quite by chance found himself in the inferno of a battlefield in 1859. He had gone to a little Apennine village to see the Emperor Napoleon III about a book he had written, but the Battle of Solferino had just taken place. The wounded were lying on the streets with no one to care for them. Dunant arrived at the moment two wounded prisoners, who had been found in a house, were thrown down the steps with curses.

"Stop!" he cried in anguish to the culprits. "Don't do that! *Sono fratelli!* [They are] brothers!"

The soldiers hesitated. They looked with surprise at this gentleman in white who seemed like a heavenly visitor.

"Sono fratelli" became a new watchword, which ran like wildfire through the little town, and a great activity began then and there. Women brought out bundles of lint. Boys carried pails of water. Dunant gave his well-filled purse to a bystander, telling him to go and buy what was needed.

Soon straw pallets lay in rows in the churches. Four Austrian doctors, one German and some Italians appeared and began the work of mercy. The Italian students, dispatched for supplies, brought a consignment of chloroform, new then in the therapeutic world. The patricians took the wounded into their houses. The Ursuline Convent became a hospital. Henri Dunant worked for three days as if in a dream. There was no end to the misery. When one poor soul was rallied back to life, another slipped into the merciful oblivion of death.

When he came to himself, Dunant had forgotten all about his book. It passed out of the picture. At once he began his long campaign of seeing influential people and telling them something must be done for the wounded in war.

During many years, he pursued his work of mercy, finding a response that gladdened his heart. But all the time he knew these efforts were of momentary value. At last he decided he would write his experiences in a book, and his *Recollections of Solferino* was published and caught public attention at once.

"Is it not possible," he wrote in his book, "to found relief societies in peacetime to care for the wounded in war, without respect to nationality? These leagues will give assistance in every time of need, pestilence, floods, fires."

Great was the response to his book. Newspapers, churches, universities gave it their blessing. Charles Dickens, in 1863, wrote a detailed analysis in his [weekly magazine] *All the Year Round,* which was read by the English-speaking world. Dunant became a popular idol. "The man in white," he was called.

Florence Nightingale was the first Samaritan on the field of battle. Dunant followed at Solferino. Clara Barton was the third in this spiritual league, which brought the humanitarian movement to the country.

The house in Geneva where the Red Cross was organized is still in use. I attended a meeting of the National Council of Women in the room and saw the brass plate that records the date of its birth in October 1863. The Red Cross was chosen for the emblem in compliment to Henri Dunant's nationality. The Swiss flag is a white cross on a red ground.

Strangely enough, evil days and misunderstandings came to Dunant, and the leadership of the work he had so gloriously founded passed into other hands. Barton had much the same experience. She, too, was dethroned and died a sadly disillusioned woman.

After the loss of his money and friends, Dunant lived in poverty. He was no longer remembered, until a humane woman, Berta von Sutter, found him and restored him to the front ranks of the great Europeans of that century.

He was thin, pale and old, but the cramped hand seized the pen again and he again sent out appeals for peace. In 1897, he addressed a warning to the world, which in the light of today sounds like an utterance of prophecy that is being fulfilled before our eyes.

He was given the Nobel Prize, but this sudden wealth, in the stiff hands of an old man who cared nothing for money, was another of life's ironies. He stayed where he was, in his humble room, and gave his prize to philanthropic societies.

If anyone ever deserved a Peace Prize, Dunant did, for it was the dream of his life that the Red Cross of the battlefields would become the Red Cross of Peace.

He died on Oct. 30, 1910, aged eighty-five, a broken-hearted man. His testament of faith was written and the long day ended.

"I want no ceremonies," he wrote. "I am a disciple of Christ, as in the first century—and nothing more."

The Red Cross has been in existence seventy-seven years. Its work for humanity goes on for poor, bleeding, maimed humanity caught in the trap of racial hatreds, greed, lust for power, ignorance and fear.

Is it enough to bind wounds and outfit the fighting men—if they are thereby merely enabled to fight again? Or is there a deeper work for this great body of unselfish people, who at this time all over the world are busy with their work of mercy? I quote from the last paragraph in this stirring book: "The Red Cross, which heals wounds, must also prevent wounds: The Red Cross which in our desolate present remains one of the few havens of humanitarianism, will also be one of the few sources from which humanitarianism may once more water the parched and ruined earth."

"WE HAVE ROOM FOR MANY MORE PEOPLE IN CANADA."

> JUNE 1, 1940

I am sure that you can do a fine service if you will study the question of refugee children. There are 9,400 of them in England right now, waiting for homes and transportation to come to Canada. I am sending you some literature.

Call in your friends and tell them about these children. Give them a talk on the whole question of refugees and our responsibility. There is a great deal of misapprehension on the subject.

Remind them that the United Empire Loyalists were refugees and look at the contribution they made to the cultural and industrial life of Canada. In 1840, many liberal-minded Germans took refuge in Canada and the United States, bringing music and culture, mechanical gifts, cleanliness and thrift.

We have room for many more people in Canada. If we deny the "right of asylum" to the disinherited people of Europe, we will surely repent in bitterness some day. While I was writing this . . . I stopped to listen to the new prime minister, who says the war aim of the Allies is victory, for without victory there will be no survival, and so he concluded, "Let us go forward together!"

I want to say that to you and to add this word—we save ourselves in direct ratio to our efforts to save others.

"LET US LOOK AT SOME OF OUR WEAK SPOTS."

When Hitler talks of the weakness of democracy, we spring to its defence—and rightly so. Democracy at its lowest ebb is better than his system of terror and force, lies and deception, but democracy at its lowest ebb will never kindle a young heart or strengthen an old one.

Let us look at some of our weak spots.

Our whole attitude toward manual labour is wrong and will have to be changed. We belie the very foundation of democracy, which is that all men are equal. Our idea of success is not service but comfort, and that craven thing will never fire any young heart to great and noble deeds.

In some way we have failed to inspire people with a love of their country, a sacrificial love. The war is helping. Now, threatened as we are, people are loosening their hold on their possessions. But a dark fear grips us. We should have done all this in time of peace!

However, we are here, alive and well. Our hearts are stirred; our eyes have been opened. Yesterday is gone, but tomorrow is ours. Democracy, which exalts the individual and allows him the privilege of choice, must win. The dream of a free people enjoying the work of their hands and uniting with all other free people in cultural pursuits which "make rich and add no sorrow" will not go down before the mechanized forces of evil.

But we have no right to blame God in our present distress. If we lose, we lose by our own weakness, complacency and love of ease. Let us get that clear!

If we had been willing to take fewer luxuries so that others might have necessities, if we had followed the Golden Rule in our daily walk and conversation, making it the charter of our liberties, we would have drawn all men and women into a glad fellowship. We would have built up a citizenry that no suave enemy could seduce.

Fascism, Nazism, Communism thrive only on discontent, hunger and frustration. Busy people, working in harmony with their neighbours, do not listen to subversive voices.

But the die is cast! The power of evil, about which we were disposed to joke a bit and flirt with when it came dressed up in pleasure's robes, now stands revealed before us. It stands before us in tanks that belch fire, in planes that drop bombs on hospitals and schools, in grasping bloodstained hands, ready to strangle the innocent and throttle our liberties.

It stands before us, too, in hired agents, ready to offer safety and high place to those who can be bribed. We believe we will conquer. We know we will eventually. We believe in the promise of a new heaven and a new Earth and we know it begins in hearts made tender.

One immediate service we can render our country is a simple one. German propaganda has been directed toward our tourist traffic. People in the United States have been told that Canada is no longer a pleasant place to visit, that our people are full of jitters and resentment, harshly critical of our neighbours to the south.

Let us write letters to our American friends, assuring them that Canada stands ready to welcome them. The roads are better than ever before, the skies are blue, the grass is green, the flowers are in bloom, the cherries are ripe, the glacier at Lake Louise has had a fresh fall of snow, and all the eating places and hotels are in readiness. Never were these two countries more closely united than at [this] time.

We do not deny that the money the tourists spend in Canada is doubly welcome this year, but there is something more. We want their friendly conversations and pleasant contact. We have always been good friends.

This year we are something more! We are comrades in a new crusade and our fellowship is something to cherish. Tell them to come and give us what the Princess Juliana [of the Netherlands] asked for—"strengthening love."

"THE NEED IS HERE, SO WE RESPOND."

> AUGUST 10, 1940

Hot summer lies over the world today, with bees droning in the lavender, robins ringed around the bird baths, blackberries ripe on their thorny branches, crows sitting quietly on fence posts, darkly brooding, and in the air gentle sounds of hoes at work while the farmers cultivate their crops to conserve the moisture.

On the road, many children in shorts, on bicycles and afoot, are on the way to a lake to swim. The water is warmer there, but the hardier ones prefer the robust tang of the salt water, cold though it may be. Last night, as we came home from town, we passed dozens of "hostellers" on their wheels, with knapsacks and bedrolls on their way to Mount Douglas Youth Hostel, where beds and shower baths await them and a place to cook their bacon.

Tomorrow being Wednesday and a half-holiday, there will be picnics at every beach and in all the parks.

"We do not want any speeches this year," I heard someone say at the committee meeting we had last week to arrange for the Alberta picnic. "We want to forget the war just for this one occasion. We want to talk about the things we laughed over in the days gone by, in the good old days when we were safe and poor and happy."

And then we forgot that we were a group of sober-minded, middle-aged people called together to arrange a picnic in wartime and went back to stories of chuckwagons and dude ranches and chinook winds that could melt snow so fast that people were afraid to drive their sleighs to town, when that pale green band was arched over the western sky.

But I began to tell my readers about the summer here at Gordon Head, the soft lavender-scented summer, brightened with the song of larks and the flashing wings of the yellow canaries and butterflies. The peaches are weighing down the branches on the tree that loops over the kitchen window like an awning. The salpiglossis are magnificent in their velvet dresses, violet, purple and crimson, veined in gold and silver, and on the ground, humble and glad, blooms the bright-faced portulaca.

The Margaret Beaton gladiolus are in bloom now, creamy white with a throat of red, prize winner last year in Chicago in the open class. It has eighteen flowers on one stem and lords it over all the flowers in the garden. Margaret Beaton is the creation of a young man in Winnipeg, Jerry Twomey, and what a source of pride it must be to him! I saw it the first year it was exhibited at a flower show and knew I was looking at royalty.

Above all this, airplanes pass singly and in formation, for this is Air Supremacy Week and all our people are air-minded. On the city street, people lay down silver coins to make up the $50,000 Victoria has promised to raise for planes.

There is a great jam-making campaign going on, too, to prevent any wastage of fruit, real community effort, all service given freely. The fruit-growers give the berries, young people pick them, the Red Cross has given a thousand pounds of sugar and women do the work. It's great fun, one busy woman told me. And this effort is duplicated in many places.

The need is here, so we respond. There will be tons of fruit done into first-class jam, owned by the Red Cross and used by them in whatever way they wish. In this way, the fruit has been saved and our consciences are kept clear and we have had fun. We should have done this every year.

The hot weather gives the suntan girls encouragement to go on with their campaign to raise Red Cross money by the simple method of not wearing stockings. I find it hard to detect any difference. The shades of skin vary, but all are beautiful and the eye is not offended. A good, smooth, well-shaped leg, hued with health, is a more beautiful sight than any piece of fabric.

When night falls, all the garden scents rise, the white nicotine and what is left of the night-scented stocks. The moon will not be up until 10:00 p.m., but I know it is worth waiting for, for with the forest fires, it will be as rich and lovely an orange as ever came out of a crate.

The California poppies gleam paper-white in the dusk. In the daytime they look like poached eggs, but at night the yellow fades out, leaving the white to glow with an inward light.

Hollyhocks sway their rosettes of pink and crimson. Their first flowers are gone but they always manage to have at least one flower on top. Eight feet high, some of them are, not always straight nor able to keep from listing, but the flag of colour still floats aloft.

They make me think of the old families who still have one son to carry the banner of freedom.

"GOD DOES NOT BALANCE HIS BOOKS EVERY SATURDAY NIGHT."

" will lose my faith if we do not win this war." Three times this week I have heard this, and I feel I must deal with it. Our people grow panicky, not from lack of courage but lack of knowledge. One thing is certain, if we, the free people, lose our faith, most certainly we shall lose the war, for faith is our strongest defence. We must cherish it, guard it, defend it as our fighting men will guard and defend our coasts.

Faith always demands a long view. God does not balance His books every Saturday night. In all departments of life it is a mistake to look for quick returns. Christ told his disciples not to look back when they put their hand to the plow, for he knew if they did they would be discouraged.

We must not sacrifice tomorrow for today, as some people seem disposed to do. It is a poor farmer who eats his seed potatoes.

I have always envied the people who are so sure we are going to win the war, just because we are the British Empire and our victory is written in the stars. This, in itself, is the good bridge that carries them high over the flood. I hope nothing will ever disturb it.

But there are many others who question and remember and are anxious. Some of them now cry out in their agony for clear definite help in this time of great need. They wonder why God does not interfere. Why He seems to sleep while His people perish.

On May 26, we had a day of prayer. We knew we needed help but we didn't know just how desperate the need was.

The next day, the evacuation from Dunkirk began and that accomplishment surely was a miracle. If the sea had been stormy and if the nights had been clear, the dangers would have been multiplied. But the sea was calm and a sheltering fog came over the channel and in these circumstances came a direct answer to our prayers.

Since the beginning of the war we have heard with dread that Germany has a secret weapon, which turned out to be the magnetic mine. The German high command believed in its invincibility. Their scientists had worked eight years to prove this, but the British found a way of annulling it in three weeks.

The whole British defence is a miracle. For seven years, Germany has starved her people to get ready for war, while England went on her peaceful way ignoring the danger, still believing in her old methods of compromise.

We are not proud now of our unawareness of danger but at least we are exonerated from the charge of having had war ambitions. Today, after all the shocks of betrayal and all the other hard blows that have fallen, the island fortress holds. That is a miracle!

But we have not yet mobilized all our people. The registration will help, but there are still undiscovered mines of strength here in Canada, people who are capable of great service, who are still unaware of the need.

In England, the government decided to dismiss all aliens from positions of trust, a procedure that seemed justifiable in the face of great danger, but as time went on the statesmen took a saner view and now there have been reinstatements. Many of the aliens were people who had left Germany because they hated the barbarous rule of Hitler. Under the first decree they were treated as spies and enemies, but now this has happily been changed.

The essence of democracy is tolerance, reason and justice. We must emphasize this. Let us tell this to our children and impress it on our friends, for it is a precious inheritance.

Too many of our people are still thrashing out old chaff, like the Irish who are still divided into Protestant and Catholic, though the enemy is at their gate. I heard a sermon recently in which England, Canada and the United States were charged with all the mistakes of the past. All the skeletons were taken from the closets and paraded before us. We had nothing left to be proud of and the sunshine of that bright Sunday morning grew pale and menacing as we listened.

If we had no inner fortification, our hearts would have been frozen with a fear that the democratic countries of the world were utter failures and did not merit survival. The speaker evidently forgot that we are at war and this is no time for recrimination and charges.

Morale is more than half the battle in times like these.

When I was in Ottawa recently, I had dinner one night in the Grill Room of the Château Laurier, a lovely room, with crystal chandeliers, banked flowers, a great dancing floor in the centre of the room and an orchestra at one end, tables all around. On the floor, dancing with a young girl, I saw an old man, in the uniform of a general, a distinguished-looking man, his face criss-crossed with wrinkles and his shoulders bent with years of intense living.

I could see that this husky young partner, probably his granddaughter, had dragged the old man away from his peaceful fireside. His knees were stiff, his feet tender. He made me think of a racehorse, grown too old for the track, but trying to get into his old stride. I could almost hear his knees squeak and I resented this brazen young woman. Why didn't she pick on someone her own age—for I know about stiff knees.

The orchestra played "I'll Never Smile Again", [and] "Night and Day, Day and Night," and still the young one pushed the old man around.

Then suddenly the music changed and the young tenor who was doing the vocals began to sing "There'll Always Be an England"

and I was a bit shocked at that. It did not seem just right. Surely that is the subject for prayer rather than for dancing.

That's what I thought. But I soon had reason to change my mind. The old general and his granddaughter passed in front of us again, and what a change had taken place! The old back had straightened, the old face was no longer old, the wrinkles were gone. His eyes had a new gleam, and his feet were light.

He was the leader now. He was swinging the young one.

[As] I looked at that fine old face, I caught the radiance, the gleam, the infectious challenge, and I sang, too. And then with one impulse we all stood up and sang and sang. And so it happened that an ordinary dinner program in a hotel dining room became a dedication service to King and Country and all that we hold dear.

We need more of this. We need more bands playing in the street, more flags flying, more coming together, more building of morale, more concern for other people. There are good old pianos in rooms not much used, where young and old people, boys and girls, sailors and soldiers, could gather on Sunday evenings, to sing hymns of the church and songs of the nation, to build up reserves of character against the evil days ahead of us.

No people ever had a better cause than we have, or a greater reason for waging war with all our might. Everything we have is in the balance. If we lose, we lose all.

So let us postpone our criticisms for a brighter day. Stop blaming other people for their neglect and failures. Let us reserve all our criticism for ourselves and look around us to see what we can do in this—man's greatest fight for freedom.

"WE WILL GET ON FASTER WITH THIS BUSINESS OF SETTING OUR HOUSE IN ORDER WHEN WE STOP RECITING OTHER PEOPLE'S SINS."

> SEPTEMBER 21, 1940

Germany has demonstrated beyond a doubt that people can be turned back to savagery by rigid discipline; they can be stripped bare of every decent human emotion and turned into machines as ruthless as the sawing-machine which at this moment is biting its way through a pile of slabs at Lantern Lane. It is the grim way that this great blade whangs through the wood that started me thinking.

There is another side to this matter of discipline. Our hearts are thrilled to hear about the children on their way to Canada, who behaved like "guardsmen on parade" when their ship was torpedoed; this also shows what can be done by training. In these cases, so widely differing, there is one common condition. A motive has to be supplied.

The German people are told that there is only one consideration in life and that is the German race. Other races must be enslaved. They must be made to feel the "triumphant sword of the overlord." Their whole plan of life is an appeal to every selfish instinct, but it works.

The British children are told that all humanity is threatened by an evil power and their only hope is in their own invincible spirit. They must be strong and brave, not only for their own good, but for the ultimate liberation of humanity. And that works, works admirably. It gives to all who accept it an elation of soul and a steadfastness of purpose.

But what about Canada? Are we still eating and drinking and going our own prodigal ways, cutting the crusts off our sandwiches, throwing away bottles, cartons, cans, tubes and enough food to feed all the people on relief, spending more money on cigarettes and liquor than we do on education and social services?

I once asked an Australian woman who visited here just before the war, what Canadian characteristic was to her the most striking. Without hesitation she said: "Your wasteful ways, especially in the matter of food. When I see people crumbling white bread on a tablecloth and leaving squares of butter on their plate, I could cry."

Now some will say in reply to this that we have great surpluses of food in Canada and if we begin to save, our surpluses will be greater. Yes, we have surpluses of food, wheat, bacon and fruit, but we also have undernourished people. We have not yet contrived sensible plans for the distribution of our stores.

The war has driven us to solve some of our problems, but there are still many that can only be solved by individual discipline. We need less talk and more action.

I get letters from my readers, many of which are helpful and thoughtful, but the great majority of them reek with abstractions. I still get letters from people who blame all our troubles on armament makers and war profiteers, the evils of party politics, lack of leaders in the church, the extravagance of women. When people take in as much territory as this, I know it would be very irritating to tell them to look around them and begin the work of redemption in their own hearts and their own homes.

We will get on faster with this business of setting our house in order when we stop reciting other people's sins. But I know that I am cutting off a pleasant zone of conversation when I say this.

We have just started the second year of the war and the end is not in sight. Canada grows in importance every day as a nation, and we as individuals must put away childish things if we are to become worthy of our great destiny.

I would like to suggest a simple exercise in this matter of discipline. Let us set a guard on our lips, remembering that the tongue is an unruly member. Let us stop wisecracking about our American neighbours.

I do not believe we really feel any antipathy toward the Americans, but we are like the people who live in the little house, near a larger and much grander house. We try to bridge the inequality by saying slighting things about the rich neighbours. Most of it is done just to make conversation, but that does not prevent heart-burnings.

I have had an American-born friend with me for some time and naturally she is sensitive on these matters, just as I was sensitive when I went to England and resented the tones of superiority when the people spoke about the colonies. We seldom go out to a public meeting or any gathering that she does not receive a thrust regarding her native land. And in such unexpected places and from such innocuous people.

A sweet-faced old grandmother rebuked her grandson when he used the word "lousy" describing the literature of his grade. "Oh Arthur," she cried in distress. "Where do you get this low American slang?"

If we must talk about the people who live in the Big House, let us tell about the numbers of their young men who came across the border to enlist in our army. Let us speak with gratitude of our good fortune in having people of our own way of life living beside us. Let us mention the fact that they have recently made provisions for a huge sum of money to help us market our surplus grain products in an orderly fashion.

Speaking of the wheat crop in Canada and the difficulties presented, I have an interesting clipping from one of the weekly newspapers of Saskatchewan, which throws some light on how one community is helping to solve this problem. The paper is called the *Comet* and is published at Radisson, Saskatchewan.

On Sunday afternoons, these people got together and talked over the problems of the district and as a result of these meetings have published a statement in the local paper. A sort of declaration of faith, which reads as follows:

1. We can be honest about the acreage we have in wheat. We can refuse to try to wangle anything for ourselves. Every time we cheat, our neighbours and our country suffer.

2. We can help each other with the storage of wheat on our farms.

3. We can protect our grain from livestock.

4. We can accept cheerfully the necessary restrictions. Cheerfulness is just as contagious as grumbling!

    We the undersigned pledge ourselves to this program as part of our contribution to the unity and strength of Canada.

A member of the Bracken Wheat Committee made the remark when he read this statement that if such a spirit prevailed in every district, the problems of western Canada could easily be solved.

The discipline these people have accepted is self-imposed. There is no spy-eye at the keyhole. Their driving force comes from their own souls. In spite of many crop failures, these are happy people who sing at their work, for their life has a plan. They know that they are part of the new spirit, which alone can bring peace and satisfaction to this harassed and troubled world.

"I AM IN THE RIGHT MOOD TODAY TO WRITE ABOUT THANKSGIVING, FOR I HAVE BEEN WRAPPING APPLES."

> OCTOBER 12, 1940

Some choleric people sneer at Thanksgiving Day, Mother's Day and all other definite cataloguing of emotions. "We should be thankful every day and love our mothers every day," they say, "and not follow the calendar in such matters."

While that is true, it is in no way disturbed by having one day in which we give expression to our loyalty and devotion. Every good housekeeper knows the value of a timetable. She washes on Monday, irons on Tuesday, sweeps on Friday, bakes on Saturday, and goes to church on Sunday. Her life is given a rhythm in this way, which saves it from confusion.

And so it is with Thanksgiving Day. It has become part of our life's pattern. We remember events in relation to Thanksgiving Day. It divides that long stretch from the first of September until Christmas.

This year Thanksgiving is especially welcome, for our hearts are torn with anxieties and fears; dark pictures haunt our minds. These words will appear in print on the Saturday before Thanksgiving Day, when the people will be busy decorating the churches with the fruits of the earth and the children's choir will be practising their songs of harvest.

Pumpkin and squash in fantastic shapes, onions and apples and pears and grapes, the finest of them, without blemish or spot, will be heaped before altars. Chrysanthemums and dahlias and marigolds will bring the sunshine into the dim light, warming it with their radiance. There will be sermons preached about the overshadowing goodness of God, and the mystery of growth.

Sadness will be there, too, as we think of the people whose fields have been defiled and whose food has been stolen from them, whose homes demolished and altars desecrated, and we will be dull clods indeed if we do not consecrate our hearts anew to do all we can to right these wrongs.

Now, following the lead of that great soul [poet] Rupert Brooke, who fell in the last war, let us think of the things that have pleased us, and thank the Giver of all good gifts. I am thankful that colour and beauty are widespread and free. The sun sets as brilliantly over a prairie farm as it does over the homes of the rich and great.

Art has ceased to be a cloistered thing confined to galleries; it appears even in the advertising pages of our magazines. I have before me the picture of a model kitchen in shades of cream, peach and rose, which stirs me like a strain of music. Who does not thrill with longing at the reconstructed attic rooms with their alcoves and dormer windows, and the seed catalogues which almost cry with colour.

Music has come to the common people, too, by the miracle of radio. I rejoice that the trapper at the Arctic Circle can hear Brahms's Lullaby and Handel's Largo, to his everlasting comfort and up-building.

I am in the right mood today to write about thanksgiving, for I have been wrapping apples, and putting them away for the winter, Kings and Wealtys, with red cheeks; and before that I stuffed a squash with chopped meat, onions and tomatoes, flavouring it with thyme and sage, and a dash of red pepper, all grown here except the meat and the pepper. (I found out something about apples, too, when I was sorting and wrapping them. The growers do not get half enough for them).

I have never outgrown the wonder that comes from planting seeds and watching them grow. To set seeds in the ground and think of the possibility of growth links us with immortality. A little girl in Vancouver heard me express a wish for seeds of that lovely vine maple which grows in the woods on the Mainland and she sent me some seeds, which I have planted now. I put earth on a brick in a pan of water, then planted the seeds in the earth. The brick will bring the water to them. There is something fascinating about planting trees.

It is the continuity of life that wraps [us] in its kindly embrace, for no one can be utterly cast down who has some link with the future. The perversion of this makes people carve their initials on trees and park benches. I am thankful today that life has a continuity and that we can plant trees which will outlive us.

I had a great throb of thanksgiving on September 23, when I heard the King's words: "I am speaking from Buckingham Palace." In spite of all that the powers of evil could contrive, the King still speaks to his people from his own house, calm words of encouragement and confidence to the forces, tender words of sympathy for the bereaved, and words of faith to all of us. After the tempest, wind and fire, came the still, small voice of calm.

We are a free people, who have not, and will not, bow the knee to Baal. And in that we rejoice with great thanksgiving and we rejoice because we have a part in this great Battle of Humanity. No nation of our size ever had a heavier responsibility. But we are measuring up to it. Something is happening in our commonplace lives. We feel our cheeks brushed by angels' wings.

Thanksgiving Day this year will not be a time of emotion only. It will be a time of Consecration.

"MANKIND WAS NOT PROMISED THE EASY LIFE OF A LOTUS EATER."

> EASTER 1941

Easter was never more needed or more welcome than it is in this Year of Trouble when everything depends on the spirit of free men and women. Easter, with its buds and flowers, its creative sources, its message of hope and victory over powers of darkness, speaks to us of the latent forces in the world—the beneficent forces which make all things new.

Like is not a vale of tears. I never liked the hymns that dwell on this dreary aspect, to make a sharp contrast between Earth and Heaven, with its streets of gold and walls of jasper. God has put great thought into the making of this world, and it is a poor compliment to Him for us to revile it. Having made man, He must know the depths to which man in his greed and vanity can fall, and He must know, too, how human society can be thrown back to decency. (I should not say brought back.) The good behaviour of mankind was of short duration. Having given man free will, God must have known He was going to have trouble.

It is not difficult to see God's physical plan for humanity. He made the world of various soils and climates so men would need each other's products; He gave us gifts differing so that we must depend on each other and learn to live together. And He made an abundant provision for everyone in raw material—ores, timber, animals, crops, beauty, everything—and above all He recognized the fact that living even with all these provisions would be difficult. Mankind was not promised the easy life of a lotus eater.

At Easter time, when the world is full of promise and beauty, it should be easy for us to believe in a New Life. Everyone craves new things in the spring; and this year, though we may not indulge our fancy in new curtains, or new hats, we can take great comfort in new ways of thought. Let us become more articulate in our desire for a better world. It is not enough to somehow hope that good will be the final goal of ill. We must be definite. We must build each other up. Sing more, visit more, write more letters, plan for other people's happiness. Think of ourselves as part of the army of defence.

When the British children leave their country for refuge in other lands, they are each given a book called *A Token of Freedom*, which contains great messages from the Bible, from Shakespeare, Milton, Tagore, Lincoln and many others who knew how to make words do their bidding. The object of this little book is to let the children see that freedom is a precious thing which has been won by sacrifices, and that no sacrifice is too great in freedom's cause; for without freedom, life has no meaning.

I wonder what sort of a Token of Freedom we are giving to our children in Canada. I thought of this when I listened to a radio quiz program recently where the contestants were all children. They were not being questioned on the cities or the rivers or writers or musicians of their country or any character in history. No, their knowledge of the comic strips was the basis of the quiz and they certainly knew all about them.

Now I am not saying a thing against the comic strips, and a good laugh is not to be despised at any time, but to make these flimsy creatures the subject of a program on the air seems like a false emphasis. Especially now when we should be preparing children of today for the sacrifices ahead. We should be giving them the best we know. Children who speak the language of the King James version, Shakespeare and Kipling should be given something more nourishing than even Popeye and his can of spinach.

Easter means much to us this year, for we are living again through the dark Friday and Saturday. Humanity in many lands is going through the agonies of cruel death and humiliating oppression. People who thought they could save themselves by neutrality have been brought to bitter desolation. The night of despair has settled down on many a heart. But the story is not ended and the night wears on toward morning. Already there are glimmerings of dawn.

"IT WAS A TYPICAL CANADIAN SCENE, EVERYONE DOING EXACTLY AS THEY WISHED AND EVERYONE HAVING A GOOD TIME."

> AUGUST 1941

This afternoon I sat in the car and watched the people enjoying a lovely afternoon in Mount Douglas Park, about six miles from Victoria. I saw children going up into the tree-tops on swings and bathers going down the steep path to the sea in their bright, brief garments; mothers marshalling their dripping offspring and getting dry clothes on them behind trees and between cars; men in shirtsleeves carrying tea, coffee or milk from the store in bright pitchers and pots—probably our own creations from the Medicine Hat Potteries, bright table-cloths on the tables on which baskets and boxes of food were waiting—picnic suppers in all stages of preparation and performance. It was a typical Canadian scene, everyone doing exactly as they wished and everyone having a good time.

A few people played shuffleboard; some sat with their backs against trees reading; older people sat in cars listening to radio programs and some just sitting, as I was. Ahead of us was the sea, still and calm, streaked with blue shadows; beyond, San Juan Island and the Washington shore; white sailboats drifted idly with the tide. Cars came in and cars went but no one directed the traffic. There was not even a sigh to tell us to pick up our papers but everything was orderly and pleasant.

Behind us under the tree stands the Mount Douglas Hostel Camp, painted green, where fifty travellers can be comfortably bedded down each night. When the bunks are full the travellers sleep under the trees. In front of the store stand great beds of petunias; on the veranda are tables where people who wish can have meals, and good ones, too. I went in to see Mrs. Edwards, the proprietor, and passed a man and woman—hostellers by their costumes—who were talking about Geneva and the International Labour office there. The hostellers have been coming and going all summer, sometimes in parties with a leader, sometimes alone. The youngest hosteller to arrive unattended this year was a thirteen-year-old girl on her bicycle.

And this is Canada, our own country, so free we never think of freedom. Let us rejoice and be glad in it!

"SOY BEANS HAVE A HISTORY."

One of the joys of living in the country is that there is always some little chore to do which gives release from the bitter problems of the world.

Soy beans have a history. Hou Tsi, one of the gods of agriculture —so say the Chinese—finding himself in an expansive mood one day decided to bestow a great gift on humanity, so he planted a soy bean. Now for a hundred generations this little bean has been a valuable food for people who are short of milk or meat.

The first soy bean came to this continent in 1804 and was then merely a botanical curiosity, but since science has discovered the soy bean it has certainly gone to town and is now used in making soap, salad oils, varnishes, paint, linoleum [and] plastics and can be mixed with wool for cloth—and that is not one-half of its uses.

Soy bean . . . pods are not easy to open by the thumbnail method but I like to do it. They are worth it. The fellowship of plants and flowers is strangely comforting when the heart is troubled. I like to think of their continuity, their unfailing rebirth, their plan for survival. All that is past points to man's survival, too.

"WE MUST NOT SINK INTO HITLER'S WAYS OF PUNISHING INNOCENT PEOPLE JUST BECAUSE WE DO NOT LIKE THEIR COUNTRY."

> JANUARY 10, 1942

Never have we had such a year of surprises and shocks, and yet never since the war began have we had such high hopes of ultimate victory. The greatest surprise has been Russia. Some heads are still dizzy after their right-about-face. We were sure after the Hitler-Stalin pact, just before the war, that there was no difference between the two dictators; but on June 22, 1941, we got our answer to that. Every day since then we have received additional proof that our judgment was faulty. We misjudged the Russians.

When we look back we can see that Russia was one jump ahead of us in intelligent evaluation of the Hitler menace. At the time of Munich, one of the Russian delegates at the League of Nations, in dark despair over what had happened, told us that Russia would have to fight Germany sooner or later. This was said by [Soviet ambassador in Stockholm] Madame Alexandra Kollontai, then and now. She was not deceived by any "peace in our time" talk, neither was the present Russian ambassador at Washington, who could not be invited to the Munich conference because Hitler refused to sit down with a Jew. In order that Hitler not be offended, Mr. Chamberlain and Mr. Daladier cold-shouldered the Russian foreign minister.

Time has a way of setting things right, and so we can see we are learning, howbeit the hard way.

As women we learned something, too, in 1941, about our place in wartime, and that has been another slow process. As early as April 1939, there was a registration of all women all across Canada. Women asked to be allowed to register for war work and consent was given by the Dominion government. The registration revealed great variety in women's experience in training. On Vancouver Island alone we found women who had made munitions, been court reporters and interpreters, private secretaries to cabinet ministers, laboratory technicians, hospital matrons, physicians, factory foremen and many other highly specialized workers. Although nothing came of this registration, women's groups all over Canada began to meet, drill and study again, and again asked to be allowed to serve. But there seemed to be a number of reasons for delay. Someone was always making a survey of something, or somebody had gone to England and would not be back for six weeks. Never once were the women bluntly refused, but they were put off. Is it any wonder their ardour cooled?

But this is our country and we have to serve it in the best possible way and we know we can't save it by knitting socks and sweaters or making sewing kits, important as these are in the matter of morale and comfort. But we can see now that even morale and comfort will not save the country. Human flesh cannot meet steel and overcome it. Hitler did say something once about "breaking barbed wire with human breasts." That may be all right for Hitler, for he doesn't care about his soldiers—he deserts, betrays and sacrifices them without a quiver.

We know now we must have tanks and planes and guns. We know, too, that the time is short and the days are evil; we are ready to give up leisure, comfort and everything to supply these for our fighting men. Strong young women, keen-witted and capable, are ready to do what they can and go where they're told without a murmur. They are not afraid of toil, sweat and tears.

We rejoice, too, that there are things that even the women who are no longer young can do. I read in a British bulletin that the salvage recovered by municipal authorities in Britain has saved the equivalent of 250 voyages across the Atlantic and is valued at $14,800.00.

On December 7, in the early morning, the scene changed with tragic suddenness and there has been a quickening of the pace ever since. Our losses have been so great that we must not think about them. Able-bodied women no longer believe they are doing their full duty by hunting up old woolens to be made into blankets or cutting stamps off letters. We know that the great need of the moment is for munitions and we know that the women of Canada can do what the women of Britain have been doing.

Edna Jaques, western Canada's beloved poetess, saw this need three months ago. She found she could no longer sit in comfort writing, although her poems have comforted many and have a definite patriotic value, not only here but in the United States and Britain as well. When Coventry was bombed she wrote a message to the brave survivors and, not knowing whether any of the newspapers had come through the destruction, sent it to the postmaster. He was so touched by her words that he wrote a reply in the same metre and the two poems appeared in the Coventry newspapers.

But now Edna Jaques is not writing poems. She is making munitions and works on the night shift. When 7:00 comes in the morning, she is tired but happy, too, for she knows she is part of Canada's defence. In her poems written since the war began her touch has been steady and sure, and her new volume, called *Aunt Hattie's Place*, is full of glory and [the] heartbreak of this time. Her "Death of a Young Aviator" is one of the truly great poems of this war. I quote the last verse:

And now for him—the Tree of
Life will bear
No bitter fruit—it will be always spring.
The almond blossom white upon

The bough,
The darting swallow ever on the wing.
Age shall not touch him where
He lies serene
In some small English field of
Budding green."

I wonder if Hitler and his associates have learned anything in 1941? Evidently they haven't yet learned that the doctrine and practice of frightfulness—*Schrecklichkeit*—which was the slogan of Atilla the Hun fifteen centuries ago, does not work. Now it has united people against him everywhere and set him and his followers outside the pale of human mercy. Hitler must be destroyed, we declare, there is no other way. Even the confirmed pacifists agree on this.

Now we have another problem that calls for clear thinking. We have in this province of British Columbia, 23,000 Japanese people, many of them natives of Canada and some of the second generation. We have an opportunity now of showing them that we do respect human rights and that democracy has a wide enough framework to give peace and security to all people of good will, irrespective of race or colour. I believe that all precautions must be taken at this time, but we must not sink into Hitler's ways of punishing innocent people just because we do not like their country. The Canadian Japanese are not to blame for the treacherous attack on Pearl Harbor or the other misdeeds of their countrymen.

One over-zealous resident of Vancouver was outraged to see a policeman, convoying Japanese children across a crowded street when "there are street corners where no policeman is in attendance." Another one of the same mentality stamped off a street car because Japanese passengers were on it. Two twelve-year-old boys set fire to a Japanese home in Seattle, endangering the lives of five American-born children, and the report said, "the boys were no doubt actuated by patriotism." Now these things do not belong to our way of life. There is a touch of the Nazi in them that we cannot tolerate.

Here is a brighter item of news that fits into our framework:

"Under the Red Cross there was sent out from the Pacific Coast recently 5,680 cans of salmon caught by Japanese fishermen and canned by the Chinese for shipment to Britain."

A great opportunity is ours today to show a kindly spirit of watchful tolerance.

Let us guard well, not only our bridges and our plants, but our good name for fair dealing. We must have precautions but not persecutions.

"LIKE GIVING MUSIC LESSONS IN A BOILER FACTORY."

Boys and girls are preparing to go back to school. You will see them buying their new books in the bookstores and you may be sure that their parents are wishing again that the school boards would buy the books or at least that the department would not so frequently change the books. But anyway the children are soon going back to school and soon school bells, with iron clang, will announce the opening of the fall term all across Canada, and in many a home as the thundering herd departs there will come a sudden silence like the stopping of a clock.

We wonder what our young people are getting in their classes that will help them to meet the future. Their parents and grandparents are no longer competent to guide them on the well-known basis of "When I was your age . . ." We were never confronted with the global complexities which face the youth of today, so before school starts it is well for us to have a look at the scene.

We hear rumours of increased juvenile delinquency, caused by the absence in war work of one parent or both. Stories come through of children wandering the streets after school hours, of women coming home from work tired and irritable, of the doubling up of families because of housing shortage, and many other complications which beat upon the lives of children.

The schools have suffered no upheaval yet in Canada. The flag still flies, the bell rings and the classes gather. I wonder if the teachers are sensitive to their great responsibility. I wonder if they know that wisdom is greater than knowledge and to prepare the child to make moral choices should be the supreme aim of all our education. There is a hard life ahead of these youngsters who flock into the classroom, carrying new books in their strong brown hands. The candles of freedom must be lighted in their souls. Not freedom for themselves alone, but freedom for all people everywhere. We talk a lot about a new world and a new order but, we know in our hearts we cannot have a new world except by developing new people, and the school beginning at Grade One is our house of hope.

There are terrible distractions to be met. Even children's hearts today are vitiated with too much excitement and hysteria. Trying to teach moral values in this high-pitched atmosphere of battle, murder and sudden death must be something like giving music lessons in a boiler factory. But it must be done and it can be done.

Children of all ages are hero worshippers, idealists and dreamers. Can we make the ways of righteousness and liberty and honour as attractive to our children as the ways of dishonour, brutality and enslavement have been made to the young Germans? Is it easier to teach children to hate than to love? Some defeatists say it is, but I believe that is a dishonouring of our humanity.

The pivotal point of all our teaching at this time must be the presentation of the good life. Is not the helping of our fellow men more thrilling than killing them? Cannot George Washington Carver, the scientist, be made as attractive as, let us say, Billy the Kid?

Listen to these grave words spoken by Walter Lippmann on the subject of education and knowledge: "In our schools and colleges we have gone far toward abandoning the idea that all education should be founded upon the deliberate training of the mind and upon a discipline in the making of moral choices. We have been told to jump over these ancient preliminaries and induct the pupil directly into the burning issues of contemporary life. This produces a little learning with no wisdom, philanthropists without philosophy and enthusiasts without religion . . . If western civilization is to survive and renew its vitality, we shall have to revive and renew our schools."

This revival and this renewal can be done in the quickest way from the top down. We need at the head of our normal schools, universities and colleges great educators and moral reformers, men and women who are not ashamed of being earnest, who can kindle a flame in the hearts of their students. If all our teachers, on the opening day of school, could catch a vision of the future and the part that their students will have to play, we would have a home defence army that would defend our highest traditions of right. And let us never forget there can be no creative, contagious right thinking that has not some sort of a religious foundation.

When I read of Hitler's onslaughts on religion my heart grows cold and heavy with the thought that he is working harder to destroy religion than we are in propagating it. We have been living in a carefree attitude of cheerful imbecility, everyone doing just about as he pleased, feeling that somehow, somewhere, there was a great generous margin of well-being that would cover any defects in our behaviour; a great balance in the bank that would take care of our overdrafts. Our most used phrase being, "Don't worry, everything will be all right." But no, we know that everything is not all right and we are wondering what the end will be.

We wonder about India and we think of all that Britain has done for India, the great irrigation schemes which have turned deserts into fertile fields and so prevented famines; the inestimable gift of internal peace which has been enjoyed these many years; how the natives have been given their rightful place in legislation and other governing bodies; and still the old bitterness is there. And there must be a cause. We wonder if we have worked as hard as we might have worked to bring about world fellowship.

We cannot plead ignorance, we have always known the remedy. Right at the heart of the universe and all around us, if we have eyes to see, there is a Divinity which keeps the stars in their places, causes the grain to sprout, grow and ripen and the flowers to spring from the soil. It is a good world, really, but for the beguilement of men whose evil thoughts and desires have brought sorrow and suffering, frustration and horror to millions of helpless and innocent people. And this has been going on for a long time. We think with humiliation and guilt of the persecution of the Jews in Germany, Mussolini's attack on the Ethiopians, and how little we did about it, either as individuals or as a nation.

And that brings us to think of some of the things which we know in our hearts at this moment are working havoc in our own people and which we, the people of Canada, could control, if we had the backbone.

This is, above all else, a war of ideas. The Nazis know this and work upon it with great success. They know how to degrade their victims and lull them into inaction . . . Here is one significant feature of that fiendish strategy. The Nazis have deliberately cultivated the habit of drink in the Polish youth, by providing little food and less milk but cheap and abundant liquor. They have rightly judged this instrument of moral ruin. Why do we shut our eyes to it? Do the teachers in the schools recognize it?

In this pitched battle between the forces of light and the forces of darkness, with the scales tipping against us, can we afford to be complacent about this evil that causes accidents, impairs efficiency and spreads confusion? We have not only ourselves to think of—

Is true Freedom but to break
Fetters for our own dear sake,
And with leathern hearts, forget
That we owe mankind a debt?
No! True Freedom is to share
All the chains our brothers wear,
And, with heart and hand, to be
Earnest to make others free!

[from "Freedom," by James Russell Lowell]

ROYAL OAK BURIAL PARK

By the end *of her tenure as a columnist, the great crusader must have known that she was looking back on life. Nellie McClung's doctors had told her she needed to rest, and that meant spending her time judiciously. Nellie had been trying for several years to write the second volume of her autobiography, a project that would pick up from her marriage to Wes, which was where* Clearing in the West: My Own Story *(published in 1935) had left off. She originally wanted to call her final book* Without Regret, *but in the end it was published as* The Stream Runs Fast: My Own Story *(1945). While the book does complete Nellie's story from her own point of view, most reviewers* commented that her warmth and humour did not come across as well they had in Clearing in the West.

Reviewer Rose S. McLaughlin, writing in the Victoria Daily Times, noted: "There is an impersonal quality about the latter third of the book which is vaguely disappointing. One would like to have heard more about her children and that bright-eyed crew to whom the book is dedicated, her grandchildren."

Later in the review McLaughlin notes, "A feeling of disappointment amounting almost to bitterness creeps in at times as Mrs. McClung reflects on the disparity between hopes and results."

Today's critics agree that Clearing in the West was a much more skilfully written book, but without The Stream Runs Fast there would be a large gap in our knowledge of Nellie McClung. There is no question that she was protective of her family's privacy, and what we do know is all we can ever know, because Florence, Nellie's only daughter, burned her mother's diaries and journals. We have no way of knowing if this was Nellie's wish or simply Florence's decision.

Nellie did, however, devote a section in The Stream Runs Fast to her eldest son's tragic suicide in February 1944. Jack perhaps never fully recovered from his experiences during the First World War. He drank heavily and was implicated in the misappropriation of government funds toward the end of his life. Nellie blamed the war for damaging her son irreparably. For months after Jack's death it seemed that neither Wes nor Nellie would ever recover. The family's strength and faith were severely tested, but they survived, changed, of course, but intact.

On Sunday, August 25, 1946, the McClungs celebrated their golden wedding anniversary. The perfect summer's day began with the family attending the regular Sunday service at St. Aidan's, the church that had come to mean so much to both Nellie and Wes. Over the years they had forged many deep friendships with members of the congregation, and in addition to being the first woman elder, Nellie was a frequent and popular speaker at the church. After the service *that morning, the family gathered for lunch at Lantern Lane, and in the afternoon friends and neighbours visited. There is no doubt that the celebration was heartfelt. Their long marriage was not without its trials and tribulations, but their commitment to each other was unwavering. Nellie once told a journalist that the day she "cut Wes from the herd" was her best day's work.*

Five years later, *on Saturday, September 1, 1951, Nellie died at home with Wes and other family members at her bedside. The following Tuesday, the Victoria* Daily Times *ran the following article:*

Mrs. McClung's Funeral Set Wednesday

WAS CHAMPION OF WOMEN'S RIGHTS

One of Canada's most widely known authors and campaigner for women's rights, Mrs. N. McClung, died Saturday at her Gordon Head home, Lantern Lane at the age of 77. She was the first woman appointed on the Board of Governors of the Canadian Broadcasting Corporation, a post she held from 1936 to 1942.

Mrs. McClung was a friend and supporter of Prime Minister William Lyon Mackenzie King.

Funeral services will be held from Metropolitan United Church, Wednesday at 3:00 with Reverend T. J. Griffiths, retired pastor of St. Aidan's, officiating, assisted by Reverend L. Clerihue. Interment will be at Royal Oak.

Mrs. McClung's name became a household word throughout the land with books such as *Sowing Seeds in Danny, Clearing in the West,* and *Leaves from Lantern Lane.*

A native of Chatsworth, Ont., Mrs. McClung went to Manitoba with her parents when she was seven. Following graduation from Normal School at

Winnipeg, she taught for five years in schoolhouses in the prairie backwoods. It was during these years that her resolution to fight for women's and children's rights was born.

She was long an advocate of women sitting in the Senate. Her name stands on a plaque with those of four other women at the entrance to the Senate Chamber at Ottawa, as a champion of women's rights.

Mrs. McClung is survived by her husband, R.W. McClung, three sons, Mark of Ottawa, Horace of Victoria, Paul of Vancouver and one daughter, Mrs. Hugh Atkinson (Florence) of Vancouver and nine grandchildren. She was predeceased a fourth son, J.W. McClung, Edmonton.

The funeral was held at the Metropolitan United Church because Nellie's beloved St. Aidan's Church didn't have the capacity to hold all those who were expected to attend. Nellie was buried at Royal Oak Burial Park, not far from her home. Wes lived on at Lantern Lane until his death in 1958. They are buried together.

The woman who had accomplished so much, who had changed the course of history, is memorialized on her grave marker with the simple epitaph, "Loved and Remembered." There's no question that the plain-spoken girl born in Ontario and raised on the Prairies would be pleased with that simplicity, but no doubt she would be equally pleased to know that her declaration, "Never retreat, never explain, never apologize, just get the thing done and let them howl," reverberates even today.

ACKNOWLEDGEMENTS

Compiling this book was a privilege, and I thank Rodger Touchie for entrusting the project to me. Thank you to Lara Kordic for improving my work with her considerable editing skills, and to Leslie Kenny for her ongoing support. Thanks also to designer Jacqui Thomas and proofreader Merrie-Ellen Wilcox.

Without the dedication that Dave Obee, Editor-in-Chief of the *Times Colonist* newspaper, has to Canadian social history, the idea for this book might not have been born.

The Sidney/North Saanich branch of the Vancouver Island Regional Library is a constant and invaluable support to me.

The members of the Nellie McClung Foundation were helpful with obscure facts and with their sheer enthusiasm for the project.

Erika Luebbe, at the Legislative Library in Victoria, was most helpful, as were the staff at the First Metropolitan United Church Archives and the Royal Oak Burial Park.

I was overwhelmed by the kindness, hospitality, and support that we received from St. Aidan's United Church and from the current owners and stewards of Nellie's beloved home, Lantern Lane, Holly Vear and David Budd.

And finally, as always, heartfelt thanks and love to my family. My daughters, Deborah and Robyn, have been involved in almost every book I've written. In addition to his unfailingly patient support, my husband, Robert, generously shared his skills as a photographer for this project.

BOOKS BY NELLIE McCLUNG

Sowing Seeds in Danny (1908)

The Second Chance (1910)

The Black Creek Stopping House (1912)

In Times Like These (1917)

Three Times and Out: A Canadian Boy's Experience in Germany (1918)

Purple Springs (1921)

When Christmas Crossed the Peace (1923)

Painted Fires (1925)

All We Like Sheep (1930)

Be Good to Yourself (1930)

Flowers for the Living (1931)

Clearing in the West: My Own Story (1935)

Leaves from Lantern Lane (1936)

More Leaves from Lantern Lane (1937)

The Stream Runs Fast: My Own Story (1945)

BIBLIOGRAPHY

Books

Dawson, Willow. *Hyena in Petticoats: The Story of Suffragette Nellie McClung.* Toronto: Puffin Books, 2011.

Gray, Charlotte. *Nellie McClung.* Toronto: Penguin Books Canada, 2008.

Hallet, Mary, and Marilyn Davis. *Firing the Heather: The Life and Times of Nellie McClung.* Saskatoon: Fifth House Publishing, 1993.

MacPherson, Margaret. *Voice for the Voiceless.* Montreal: XYZ Publishing, 2003.

McClung, Nellie L. *Leaves from Lantern Lane.* Toronto: Thomas Allen Publishers, 1936.

——. *More Leaves from Lantern Lane.* Toronto: Thomas Allen Publishers, 1937.

——. *The Stream Runs Fast: My Own Story.* Toronto: Thomas Allen Publishers, 1945.

Millar, Nancy. *The Famous Five: A Pivotal Moment in Canadian Women's History.* Cochrane, AB: Deadwood Publishing, 2003.

Savage, Candace. *Our Nell: A Scrapbook of Nellie L. McClung.* Saskatoon: Western Producer Prairie Books, 1979.

Periodicals

Brown, Barbara. "Friendly Neigbourhood St. Aidan's Approaches 100th Birthday." *The Daily Colonist*, September 30, 1973.

Smith, Jara. "Why St. Aidan's?" *The Islander*, November 1984.

"A Transfiguration." *The Western Recorder*, December 1933.

"Famous Five Posthumously Appointed to the Senate." *The Star*, October 8, 2009.

The following columns included in this book originally appeared in the Victoria *Daily Times* and have been reprinted in recent years by the Victoria *Times Colonist*.

"Things have a dreadful permanence when people die."
July 24, 1937

"And she would know what the larks were singing about."
April 16, 1938

"The times are brittle." April 23, 1938

"So, what more do they want?" June 11, 1938

"This was every woman's concern." June 18, 1938

"But nothing spoiled the sunshine of yesterday." March 11, 1939

"By clothes I mean not merely covering, but adornment."
July 9, 1938

"She is a radical, really." July 30, 1938

"Sea and sky and green meadow, with cattle on the land, and ships on the sea." August 27, 1938

"There is something about the sea that loosens people's tongues and draws them into a close fellowship." September 24, 1938

"What is wrong with young Canada that it will not do anything heroic for its country's good?" November 26, 1938

"Let the hurricane roar! The kale has no fears, with its tough fibre." December 3, 1938

"Every free nation, every nation which values freedom, will ever be indebted to these stout-hearted people." January 20, 1940

"A boy of the farm who would have been a producer, a builder, a sower of crops." January 27, 1940

"That cry for leaders is an old excuse. What we need today are followers." March 16, 1940

"Canadians, I believe, are beginning to stir in their sleep." April 13, 1940

"Is it enough to bind wounds and outfit the fighting men—if they are thereby merely enabled to fight again?" May 4, 1940

"We have room for many more people in Canada." June 1, 1940

"The need is here, so we respond." August 10, 1940

"God does not balance his books every Saturday night." August 17, 1940

"We will get on faster with this business of setting our house in order when we stop reciting other people's sins." September 21, 1940

"I am in the right mood today to write about thanksgiving, for I have been wrapping apples." October 12, 1940

"It is no disgrace to be 'ladylike.'" November 16, 1940

Online

CBC Digital Archives. "1929: Women Become Persons." cbc.ca/
archives/entry/1929-women-become-persons

The Nellie McClung Foundation. ournellie.com

INDEX

ABOUT THE AUTHOR

Barbara Smith was born and raised in Toronto and lived most of her life in Edmonton before settling in the Victoria area in 2006. Barbara is a full-time writer whose work is inspired by a love of mystery combined with a lifelong interest in social history. She has published over thirty books, twenty of which are collections of ghost stories inspired by true events, including *Campfire Stories of Western Canada* (a BC bestseller), *The Mad Trapper*, and perennial bestsellers *Ghost Stories of Alberta*, *Ghost Stories and Mysterious Creatures of British Columbia*, *Ghost Stories of the Rocky Mountains*, and *Canadian Ghost Stories*. Barbara was also featured on the Discovery Channel's *Hunt for the Mad Trapper*. She lives in Sidney, BC.

DISCOVER OVER THIRTY SPOOKY STORIES
SET ACROSS WESTERN CANADA!

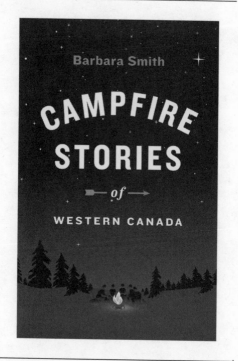

ISBN 978-1-77203-112-6 / $12.95
heritagehouse.ca